Copyright © 2024 by Marco Colombo.

All rights reserved. No part of this book may be used or reproduced in any form whatsoever without written permission except in the case of brief quotations in critical articles or reviews.

Book design by Marco Colombo
Cover design by Marco Colombo (Background Image by kjpargeter on Freepik)

THE OPTION TRADER'S INCOME BLUEPRINT

UNLEASH THE POWER OF ADVANCED INCOME STRATEGIES

VOLUME 2

UNLEASH THE POWER OF ADVANCED INCOME STRATEGIES

ABOUT THE AUTHOR

I am delighted to present to you my latest work, a comprehensive guide to mastering option income strategies. As an experienced professional with a multifaceted background in finance, academia, and investing, I bring a wealth of knowledge and practical insights to this book. Allow me to share a bit about my journey and the expertise that underpins this endeavor.

Professional Background

My career spans several years in the banking sector, where I have held various influential roles, mainly in credit risk management area. My deep understanding of the financial markets was further enriched during my tenure as a capital markets and financial sector consultant. This role allowed me to work closely with industry leaders, providing strategic advice and innovative solutions to complex financial challenges.

Academic Contributions

In addition to my professional experience, I have had the privilege of serving as a professor of statistics and probability at a prestigious university in Italy. Teaching has always been a passion of mine, and through this role, I have been able to inspire and educate the next generation of financial experts. My academic background ensures that the concepts presented in this book are not only practical but also grounded in robust statistical and probabilistic theories.

Investing Experience

Beyond my professional and academic pursuits, I am an avid investor with a diverse portfolio. My real estate investments have provided me with a solid foundation in asset management and long-term financial planning. As a retail investor and trader, particularly in options, I have developed and honed strategies that consistently generate income, even in volatile market conditions.

Purpose of the Book

This book is the culmination of my experiences and knowledge, distilled into a practical guide for anyone looking to harness the power of option income strategies. Whether you are new to options trading or an experienced trader seeking to refine your approach, this book offers valuable insights and step-by-step guidance to help you succeed.

I invite you to embark on this journey with me as we explore the intricacies of options trading and unlock the potential for steady income. With a blend of theoretical knowledge and practical application, this book aims to equip you with the tools and confidence needed to thrive in the world of options trading.

Thank you for your interest in my work. I am confident that the strategies and insights shared in this book will be a valuable addition to your investment toolkit, helping you achieve your financial goals.

DISCLAIMER AND DISCLOSURE

General Disclaimer

The information contained in this series of books, *The Option Trader's Income Blueprint*, is intended for educational purposes only. It is not intended as financial or investment advice, and the author is not a licensed financial advisor. The content provided is based on the author's personal experiences, extensive research, and knowledge gained from various courses and industry analyses. While every effort has been made to ensure the accuracy of the information presented, the author and publisher make no warranties, either express or implied, about the completeness, accuracy, reliability, suitability, or availability of the information, products, services, or related graphics contained in this book for any purpose. Any reliance you place on such information is therefore strictly at your own risk.

Investment Risks

Options trading involves significant risk and is not suitable for every investor. It is possible to lose all or more of your initial investment. Prior to trading options, you should be aware of the risks involved, including the risk of losing your entire investment. It is important to be fully informed about the specific risks associated with trading options and to understand the terms and conditions of your investments. The strategies discussed in this book are designed to generate income, but like all investment strategies, they carry risk. Historical performance is not indicative of future results.

No Financial Advice

The content of this book should not be construed as financial or investment advice. The author does not provide personalized investment advice and is not a qualified licensed investment advisor. The strategies and opinions expressed in this book are solely those of the author and do not constitute specific recommendations or advice for any individual investor. Readers are encouraged to seek professional advice tailored to their individual needs and circumstances before making any investment decisions.

Research and Sources

This book is a collection of in-depth analyses and insights derived from various courses, research, and the author's personal experiences. The material presented, including stock and option prices, has been carefully researched and compiled to provide accurate and valuable information to the reader. However, the dynamic nature of the financial markets means that the information, particularly the specific stock and option prices discussed, may become outdated or less relevant over time. Readers are encouraged to stay informed about the latest market developments, price movements, and to continue their own research beyond the scope of this book to ensure their strategies remain effective.

Personal Responsibility

The strategies and techniques outlined in this book require careful consideration and are to be used at the reader's own risk. The author and publisher disclaim any liability for any direct, indirect, consequential, or incidental losses or damages arising from the use of the information contained in this book. It is the responsibility of the reader to independently verify the information presented and to make informed decisions based on their own judgment and due diligence.

Acknowledgements

The author acknowledges the contributions of various educational courses, industry research, and personal experiences that have enriched the content of this book. The sharing of these insights aims to provide a comprehensive and practical guide to options trading, drawing from a wide range of resources and expertise.

By reading this book, you agree to the terms of this disclaimer and disclosure. Thank you for your understanding and for joining this journey into the world of options trading.

TABLE OF CONTENTS

Introduction: Unlocking the Power of Option Income Strategies 10
    Purpose 10
    Overview 12
    Your Journey to Financial Success 14

Chapter 1: Advanced Income Strategies 15
    1.1 Vertical Credit Spreads – A Strategic Approach to Income 15
    1.2 Iron Condors – Profit from Range-Bound Markets 24
    1.3 Iron Butterflies – A Precision Income Strategy 31
    1.4 Ratio Spreads – Balancing Risk and Reward 38
    1.5 Short Strangles – Profiting from Stability 44
    1.6 Short Straddles – Profiting from Stability 52
    1.7 Collar - A Balanced Approach to Risk Management 58

Chapter 2: The Ultimate Cheat Sheet: Comparing Top Option Income 63
    2.1 Summary Cheat Sheet 63

Chapter 3: Stock Repair Strategy 67
    3.1 The Purpose of the Stock Repair Strategy 67
    3.2 Step-by-Step Guide to Executing the Stock Repair Strategy 69
    3.3 Adjusting the Stock Repair Strategy 71
    3.4 Estimating Capital Requirements 71
    3.5 Conclusion 72

Chapter 4: The Wheel Strategy – Turning Opportunities into Income 73
    4.1 The Purpose of The Wheel Strategy 74
    9.2 Step-by-Step Guide to Executing the Wheel Strategy 76
    4.3 Adjusting the Wheel Strategy 82

4.4 Estimating Capital Requirements 89

4.5 Case Study – Wheel Strategy on MSFT 89

4.6 Conclusion 90

Chapter 5: LEAPS Options – Enhancing Your Strategy with Long-Term Leverage 92

5.1 The Purpose of LEAPS 92

5.2 Why Use LEAPS Instead of the Underlying Stock? 93

5.3 How to Use LEAPS in Your Trading Strategy 94

5.4 Managing LEAPS Positions 95

5.5 Practical Considerations and Examples 96

5.6 Conclusion 97

Chapter 6: Alternative Wheel Strategy with Credit Spreads 98

6.1 The Purpose of the Wheel Strategy with Credit Spreads 98

6.2 Step-by-Step Guide to Executing the Alternative Wheel Strategy with Credit Spreads 101

6.3 Adjustments and Management 105

6.4 Estimating Capital Requirements 105

6.5 Conclusion 105

Chapter 7: Alternative Wheel Strategy with Ratio Spreads 106

7.1 The Purpose of the Wheel Strategy with Ratio Spreads 106

7.2 Step-by-Step Guide to Executing the Alternative Wheel Strategy with Credit Spreads 110

7.3 Adjustments and Management 113

7.4 Estimating Capital Requirements 113

7.5 Conclusion 114

Chapter 8: Wheel Strategies: a Comprehensive Comparison 115

8.1 Wheel Strategies Comparison 115

Conclusion: Harnessing the Power of Option Income Strategies 118

Glossary 121

Table of Figures 138

Table of Tables 139

Bibliography **140**

INTRODUCTION

UNBLOCKING THE POWER OF OPTION INCOME STRATEGIES

Imagine starting each day with the assurance that your investments are working tirelessly, providing a consistent income stream regardless of market fluctuations. Envision attaining financial freedom, not just through traditional stock dividends, but through a powerful yet often misunderstood tool: options. This scenario is not merely a dream but a reality that many traders have achieved by mastering option income strategies.

Options trading offers a unique opportunity to generate reliable income, providing a way to enhance your financial future beyond the limitations of conventional investments. Many traders have found financial success through options, leveraging these instruments to create consistent income streams. However, mastering options trading is a journey that demands a solid understanding of the fundamentals, disciplined risk management, and the ability to adapt to changing market conditions.

This journey isn't without its challenges, but with the right knowledge and strategies, it is one that can lead to profound financial independence. By dedicating yourself to learning and applying the principles of options trading, you too can unlock the potential for consistent, reliable income.

PURPOSE

The Option Trader's Income Blueprint is a comprehensive series designed to equip you with the knowledge, strategies and quantitative methods needed to master the world of options trading. Whether you are a novice eager to explore the possibilities of generating income through options or an experienced trader looking to refine your skills, this series has been meticulously crafted to serve as your ultimate guide.

Options trading can be both rewarding and complex, with a steep learning curve that often deters beginners and challenges even seasoned traders. Recognizing this, *The Option Trader's Income Blueprint* is divided into multiple volumes, each focusing on specific aspects of options trading. By breaking down the material into manageable, topic-focused books, this series ensures that you build a solid foundation before progressing to more advanced strategies.

Each volume in this series addresses a particular facet of options trading, from the basics of understanding options and market dynamics to advanced strategies that can help you consistently generate income. At the time of writing, here's how the series is structured (additional volumes can be potentially added in the future):

- **[Volume 1] Master the Art of Greeks, Covered Calls and Cash Secured Puts:** This volume introduces the essential concepts of options trading, focusing on understanding the Greeks, and mastering foundational income strategies like covered calls and cash-secured puts. You'll learn how to use these tools to generate consistent income while managing risk effectively.

- **[Volume 2] Unleash the Power of Advanced Income Strategies:** Delve into more sophisticated options strategies designed to enhance your income potential. This book covers advanced techniques such as spreads, straddles, iron condors and many others, offering insights on how to implement these strategies to maximize returns. Systematic strategies like the Wheel and its alternative versions will be clearly described together with real examples.

- **[Volume 3] Strategic Adjustments and Quantitative Risk Management:** This title focuses on refining your trading strategies by making strategic adjustments and applying quantitative risk management principles. Learn how to adapt your positions in response to market changes and protect your portfolio from unforeseen risks.

- **[Volume 4] Tools and Market Strategies for a Thriving Options Business:** Explore the tools and market strategies that are essential for building and sustaining a successful options trading business. From selecting the right trading platforms to understanding market trends, this book equips you with the knowledge needed to thrive in the options market.

The series of books is designed so that each volume can stand on its own with internal consistency. However, for the best experience and a deeper understanding of the overarching narrative, it is recommended to read the books in sequential order. Each volume builds on the last, ensuring that your knowledge deepens as you progress through the series, culminating in a comprehensive mastery of options trading. By the time you complete this series, you will have gained not only a thorough understanding of options trading but also the confidence and practical skills to apply these strategies effectively in real-world scenarios.

The Option Trader's Income Blueprint is more than just a collection of books; it's a strategic pathway to financial independence through options trading. So, get ready to embark on this journey, and let's begin by laying the foundation that will support your future success in the options market.

OVERVIEW

Throughout the chapters of this book, you will embark on a comprehensive journey designed to equip you with advanced income strategies that will enhance your trading arsenal. Here's a brief outline of what you will learn:

- **Advanced Income Strategies** This chapter delves into a variety of sophisticated options strategies that aim to generate consistent income while managing risk. You'll explore vertical credit spreads, a fundamental technique for collecting premium with defined risk. The chapter then moves to Iron Condors and Iron Butterflies, which are precision strategies that combine multiple spreads to profit from low volatility. Ratio Spreads are introduced as a method to balance risk and reward by using an asymmetric spread structure. The chapter also covers Short Strangles and Short Straddles, strategies that capitalize on stable markets, and concludes with the Collar strategy, offering a balanced approach to risk management by combining stock ownership with options.

- **The Ultimate Cheat Sheet: Comparing Top Option Income Strategies** In this concise chapter, you'll find a summary cheat sheet that provides a quick comparison of the various option income strategies discussed throughout the book. This easy-to-reference guide highlights key aspects, pros and cons, and ideal market conditions for each strategy, enabling you to make informed decisions about which approach best suits your trading goals.

- **Stock Repair Strategy** This chapter focuses on the Stock Repair Strategy, a powerful technique for recovering from losing stock positions without additional capital outlay. You'll learn about the purpose of this strategy, how to execute it step-by-step, and how to make adjustments based on market conditions. The chapter also includes a discussion on capital requirements and concludes with practical insights to help you implement this strategy effectively.

- **The Wheel Strategy – Turning Opportunities into Income** Here, the Wheel Strategy is examined in depth as a method for generating income by systematically selling cash-secured puts and covered calls. The chapter guides you through the purpose of the strategy, provides a detailed step-by-step execution plan, and discusses how to adjust the strategy as market conditions evolve. Capital requirements are estimated, and the chapter concludes with a case study on Microsoft (MSFT) to illustrate the strategy in action.

- **LEAPS Options – Enhancing Your Strategy with Long-Term Leverage** This chapter introduces Long-Term Equity Anticipation Securities (LEAPS), which are long-dated options that can enhance your trading strategy by providing leverage over an extended period. You'll discover why LEAPS can be a better alternative to holding the underlying stock, how to integrate them into your trading plan, and how to manage LEAPS positions.

- **Alternative Wheel Strategy with Credit Spreads** In this chapter, the Wheel Strategy is modified by incorporating credit spreads, offering a capital-efficient way to generate income while limiting risk. You'll learn the purpose of this alternative approach, how to execute it with a detailed step-by-step guide, and how to manage and adjust the strategy as needed.

- **Alternative Wheel Strategy with Ratio Spreads** This chapter further refines the Wheel Strategy by introducing ratio spreads, which can enhance profit potential while controlling risk. You'll explore the purpose of this strategy variation, receive detailed guidance on execution, and learn how to manage and adjust positions as market conditions change. The chapter also covers capital requirements, helping you to assess the feasibility and benefits of using ratio spreads within the Wheel Strategy framework.

- **Wheel Strategies: A Comprehensive Comparison** The final chapter offers a thorough comparison of the various Wheel Strategy variations discussed in the book, including the standard Wheel Strategy, the Wheel with Credit Spreads, and the Wheel with Ratio Spreads. This comparison covers key factors such as strategy goals, risk management, capital requirements, and profit expectations, providing you with a clear understanding of which variation may best align with your trading objectives and market outlook.

Your Journey to Financial Success

As you embark on this journey, remember that the path to financial success through options trading is not without its challenges. It requires dedication, continuous learning, and a disciplined approach. However, the rewards—both financial and personal—are well worth the effort.

The Option Trader's Income Blueprint is your essential guide to unlocking the potential of options for generating steady income.

By the end of this book, you will have a deep understanding of advanced option income strategies, including vertical spreads, Iron Condors, and the Wheel Strategy, as well as specialized tactics like LEAPS and ratio spreads. Through practical advice, real-life examples, and detailed step-by-step guides, this volume will arm you with the expertise needed to generate consistent income and manage risk effectively in the options market.

Take the first step toward mastering these powerful strategies and unlocking the full potential of options trading for your financial future.

CHAPTER 1

ADVANCED INCOME STRATEGIES

1.1 Vertical Credit Spreads – A Strategic Approach to Income

Imagine being able to generate consistent income from the stock market without having to predict whether a stock will go up or down. This is the allure of vertical credit spreads—a strategic options trading approach that offers a balanced mix of risk and reward. By selling and buying options at different strike prices, traders can create positions that benefit from the passage of time and favorable price movements. This chapter will delve deeply into vertical credit spreads, providing a step-by-step guide to executing trades, setting up positions, making adjustments, and estimating the required capital.

1.1.1 The Purpose of Vertical Spreads

A vertical credit spread is an options strategy involving the simultaneous purchase and sale of options of the same type (both calls or both puts) with different strike prices but the same expiration date. This strategy is primarily used to generate income and manage risk.

- **Call Spread**: Involves selling a call option at a lower strike price and buying another call option at a higher strike price.

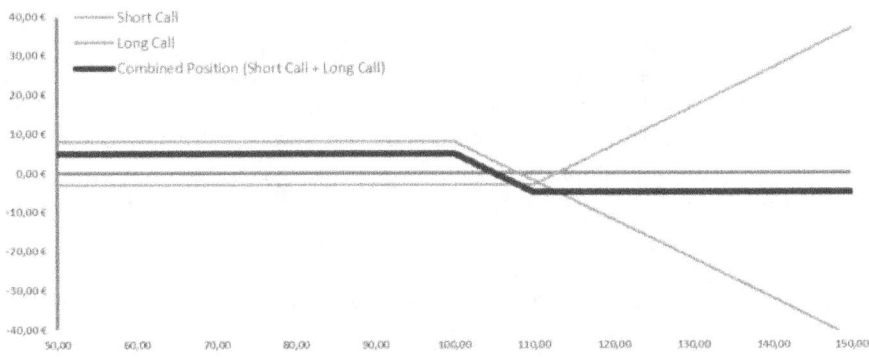

Figure 1 - Call Spread Payoff

- **Put Spread**: Involves selling a put option at a higher strike price and buying another put option at a lower strike price.

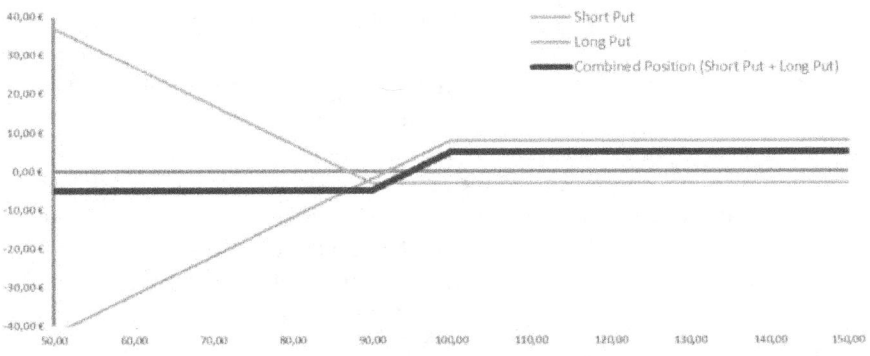

Figure 2 - Put Spread Payoff

Example: Suppose you are moderately bullish on XYZ Corp, which is currently trading at $50. You could execute a bull put spread by selling a put with a strike price of $45 and buying a put with a strike price of $40, both expiring in one month. This strategy would generate a credit upfront and would benefit as long as XYZ Corp stays above $45 by expiration.

1.1.2 Step-by-Step Guide to Executing a Vertical Credit Spread

- **Choosing the Right Underlying Asset**: Choosing the right underlying stock is crucial. Look for stocks with solid fundamentals, moderate volatility, and clear support/resistance levels. The ideal candidates are stocks with predictable price movements and favorable technical setups.
  Example: You identify ABC Inc., which has been trading within a range of $100 to $110. Without earnings or other corporate events coming up, you expect the stock to stay within this range, making it an ideal candidate for a vertical credit spread.

- **Setting Up the Trade:** The trade setup involves selecting the strike prices, expiration date, and ensuring the options have sufficient liquidity.
    - **Delta**: Choose options with a delta that aligns with your market outlook. For example, in a bull put spread, you might sell a put with a delta around -0.30 and buy a put with a delta around -0.10.
    - **DTE (Days to Expiration)**: Select an expiration date that provides a balance between premium decay and time for the trade to work. Typically, 30 to 60 days to expiration is a good range.

  Example: For ABC Inc., you decide to set up a bull put spread with the following details:
    - Sell the $100 put (delta -0.30)
    - Buy the $95 put (delta -0.10)
    - Expiration: 45 days

- **Executing the Trade:** Execute the trade through your brokerage platform by simultaneously entering orders to sell and buy the options at the chosen strike prices. Ensure the orders are linked as a spread to avoid partial fills.
  Example: You place an order to sell the $100 put and buy the $95 put, ensuring the net credit received is $1.00 per share or $100 per contract.

1.1.3 Managing Vertical Credit Spreads

- **Monitoring the Trade:** Keep a close eye on the underlying stock's price movements, implied volatility changes, and the passage of time. Adjustments may be necessary if the stock moves significantly against your position.

- **Adjusting the Spread:** Adjustments can help manage risk or lock in profits. Common adjustments include rolling up or down, closing the spread early, or converting the spread into a different strategy.
  Example: If ABC Inc. drops to $98 shortly after you enter the trade, you might consider rolling down the spread to lower strike prices. You could close the existing spread and open a new one by selling the $95 put and buying the $90 put, extending the expiration if necessary.

- **Exiting the Trade:** Exiting a vertical credit spread can be done by closing both legs of the spread simultaneously. This can be done to lock in profits or to cut losses if the trade goes against you.
  Example: If ABC Inc. remains above $100 as expiration approaches, the value of the spread will decrease. You can close the trade early to capture most of the profit or let it expires worthless if you're comfortable with the risk.

1.1.4 Adjusting Vertical Credit Spreads

Adjusting a vertical credit spread is a crucial skill for options traders. It helps manage risk, lock in profits, and adapt to changing market conditions. Here, we'll delve deeper into various adjustment methods, providing clear and detailed descriptions, real-life examples, and strategic considerations for each approach.

- **Rolling the Spread:** Rolling involves closing the current vertical spread and opening a new one with different strike prices or expiration dates. This adjustment can help manage risk, extend the duration of the trade, or align the position with new market expectations. Rolling up or down involves adjusting the strike prices of the spread to align with the new market outlook. Rolling up refers to moving to higher strike prices, while rolling down refers to moving to lower strike prices. Rolling out means extending the expiration date. You should roll a spread aiming:

- To move the strike prices away from the current price of the underlying asset.
- To extend the trade's duration and give it more time to become profitable.
- To adjust for a change in market outlook.
- To manage risk when the underlying asset moves significantly.
- To maintain a favorable risk/reward profile.

Example: You have a bull put spread on XYZ Corp, with the stock trading at $100:
- Sold the $95 put, bought the $90 put, expiring in 30 days.

If XYZ drops to $94, you might roll the spread to avoid assignment:
- Close the current spread: Buy back the $95 put, sell the $90 put.
- Open a new spread: Sell the $90 put, buy the $85 put, with an expiration 60 days out.

Example: You have a bear call spread on JKL Corp, trading at $75:
- Sold the $80 call, bought the $85 call.

If JKL drops to $70, you might roll down to capture additional premium:
- Close the current spread: Buy back the $80 call, sell the $85 call.
- Open a new spread: Sell the $75 call, buy the $80 call.

- **Converting the Position into Iron Condor / Iron Butterfly:** Converting a vertical spread into another strategy, such as an iron condor or an iron butterfly (see next paragraphs for detailed info about the strategies), can help manage risk and potentially enhance the reward profile. You should convert a spread aiming:
    - To adapt to a neutral or range-bound market outlook.
    - To capitalize on additional premium income.
    - To hedge against potential adverse movements.

Example: You have a bear call spread on DEF Inc., trading at $50:
- Sold the $55 call, bought the $60 call.

If DEF starts to range between $48 and $52, you might convert to an iron condor:
- Add a bull put spread: Sell the $45 put, buy the $40 put.

- **Selling an Additional Call or Put:** Adjusting a credit spread by selling an additional call or put is an advanced strategy that traders can use to either hedge their existing position or enhance potential returns. This approach can be particularly useful when the market is moving against the original spread, and the trader wants to adjust the risk-reward profile of the trade.

- **Adjusting a Bull Put Spread by Selling a Call***:* If the underlying asset begins to decline, you can sell a call option at a strike price near the current price of the underlying asset to offset some of the potential losses from the put spread. This transforms your position into a short straddle or a short strangle, depending on the strike prices.
  *Example***:**
    - Original Position: You have a bull put spread on XYZ stock, selling a $50 put and buying a $45 put.
    - Adjustment: XYZ stock drops to $48, and you sell a $50 call to create a short straddle.
    - Outcome: The premium received from selling the call offsets some losses from the put spread. However, if XYZ rises above $50, the call option may result in additional losses.

  This strategy generates additional premium, reducing the net loss of the position and it can be profitable if the stock remains near the strike price of the sold call and put. Anyway, it can significantly increase risk, particularly if the stock reverses direction and therefore requires careful monitoring.

- **Adjusting a Bear Call Spread by Selling a Put***:* If the underlying asset begins to rise, you can sell a put option at a strike price near the current price of the underlying asset to offset some of the potential losses from the call spread. This transforms your position into a short straddle or short strangle, depending on the strike prices.
  *Example***:**
    - Original Position: You have a bear call spread on XYZ stock, selling a $55 call and buying a $60 call.

- Adjustment: XYZ stock rises to $57, and you sell a $55 put to create a short straddle.
- Outcome: The premium received from selling the put offsets some losses from the call spread. However, if XYZ drops below $55, the put option may result in additional losses.

This strategy generates additional premium, reducing the net loss of the position and it can be profitable if the stock remains near the strike price of the sold call and put. Anyway, it can significantly increase risk, especially if the stock reverses direction and therefore it requires careful monitoring.

- **Selling an Out-of-the-Money Call or Put:** Similarly to what was discussed in the previous paragraph, if you want to limit the additional risk while still generating premium, you can sell an out-of-the-money (OTM) call or put instead of an at-the-money option. This adjustment allows you to collect premium with a lower risk of the new option being in the money at expiration.
  - Choose an OTM Strike Price: Select a strike price that is out of the money, based on your market outlook and risk tolerance.
  - Sell the OTM Option: Sell the OTM call or put to generate additional premium without taking on too much risk.
  - Monitor the Position: Regularly monitor the position to manage any potential risks if the market moves significantly.

Example:
- Original Position: You have a bull put spread on XYZ stock, selling a $50 put and buying a $45 put.
- Adjustment: XYZ stock drops to $48, and you sell a $55 call (OTM) to collect premium without taking on excessive risk.
- Outcome: The premium received from selling the OTM call helps reduce losses, but if the stock reverses, the risk is limited compared to selling an ATM call.

This strategy reduces risk compared to selling an at-the-money option, while still generation additional premium to offset losses (even if the premium collected is lower than selling an at-the-money option). It requires careful monitoring and management.

- **Closing the Spread:** Closing a vertical credit spread early involves unwinding both legs of the spread before expiration to lock in profits or cut losses. You should close early the spread aiming to:
    - To capture profits before expiration.
    - To avoid potential losses due to sudden market movements.
    - To free up capital for other trades.

Example: You have a bull put spread on GHI Corp, trading at $120:
- Sold the $115 put, bought the $110 put.

If GHI stays above $115 and the spread value drops significantly, you might close the trade:
- Buy back the $115 put, sell the $110 put, locking in most of the profit.

1.1.5 Estimating the Required Capital

Vertical credit spreads require margin, which varies depending on the brokerage. The margin requirement is typically the difference between the strike prices multiplied by the number of contracts, less the net credit received.

Example: For the ABC Inc. bull put spread ($100/$95), the difference between the strikes is $5. If you received a $1 credit, the margin required would be $5 - $1 = $4 per share or $400 per contract.

A trader can calculate the potential ROI by comparing the net credit received to the margin required.

Example: If you receive $100 credit per contract and the margin required is $400, the potential ROI is $100 / $400 = 25%.

Always consider the maximum risk, which is the difference between the strike prices less the net credit received. Ensure this aligns with your risk tolerance and trading plan.

1.1.6 Conclusion

Vertical credit spreads offer a strategic approach to income generation in options trading. By understanding the trade setup, monitoring delta and time decay, and knowing how to adjust and manage spreads, traders can effectively use this strategy to enhance their trading performance.

Incorporating vertical credit spreads into your trading plan provides a balanced approach to risk and reward, allowing for consistent income while managing potential losses. As you gain experience with this strategy, you will develop the skills and confidence needed to navigate the options market successfully.

1.2 IRON CONDORS – PROFIT FROM RANGE-BOUND MARKETS

Iron condors are a sophisticated options strategy that can provide consistent income in a range-bound market. This chapter delves deeply into the mechanics of iron condors, offering detailed, step-by-step instructions on executing these trades, setting them up with appropriate deltas and days to expiration (DTE), making necessary adjustments, and estimating the required capital. By the end of this chapter, you'll have a thorough understanding of how to implement and manage iron condors effectively.

1.2.1 The Purpose of Iron Condors

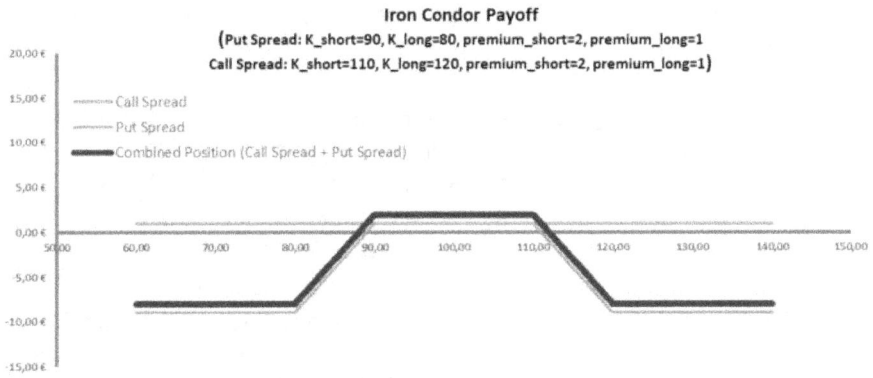

Figure 3 - Iron Condor Payoff

An iron condor is a market-neutral options strategy that profits from low volatility and time decay. This strategy involves selling an out-of-the-money call spread and an out-of-the-money put spread, both with the same expiration date. The goal is for the underlying asset to remain within the range of the sold strikes, allowing both spreads to expire worthless and enabling the trader to keep the net premium received.

An iron condor consists of four options:

- **Short Call (Sell Call):** A call option sold at a higher strike price.

- **Long Call (Buy Call):** A call option bought at an even higher strike price.

- **Short Put (Sell Put):** A put option sold at a lower strike price.

- **Long Put (Buy Put):** A put option bought at an even lower strike price.

The strategy gets its name from the shape of the profit and loss (P&L) graph, which resembles a bird with wings spread wide. The highest profit potential is the net premium received, which occurs if the underlying asset's price stays between the short call and short put strike prices at expiration. The maximum loss is limited to the difference between the strike prices of the spreads minus the net premium received.

Example: Constructing an Iron Condor

Let's consider a practical example using a hypothetical stock, ABC Inc., currently trading at $100. We anticipate that ABC will trade in a relatively narrow range over the next month due to low market volatility and no significant upcoming news events.

- **Selecting Strike Prices:** We choose the following strike prices:
    - Sell 1 Call at $110 (Short Call)
    - Buy 1 Call at $115 (Long Call)
    - Sell 1 Put at $90 (Short Put)
    - Buy 1 Put at $85 (Long Put)

- **Calculating Premiums:** Assume the following premiums for each option:
    - Sell 1 Call at $110: $2.00 premium received
    - Buy 1 Call at $115: $0.50 premium paid
    - Sell 1 Put at $90: $2.00 premium received
    - Buy 1 Put at $85: $0.50 premium paid

- **Calculating Net Premium:** The net premium received is calculated as:
    - Net Premium= (Premium Short Call−Premium Long Call)+(Premium Short Put−Premium Long Put)
    - Net Premium=(2.00−0.50)+(2.00−0.50)=3.00

- **Determining Maximum Potential Loss:** The maximum potential loss is the difference between the strike prices of one of the spreads, minus the net premium received:
    - Maximum Potential Loss=(Difference between Strikes)−Net Premium
    - Maximum Potential Loss=(5.00−3.00)=2.00

For one contract (100 shares), the maximum potential loss is: 100×2.00=$200

- **Determining Maximum Profit and Breakeven Points:**
    - Maximum Profit: Net premium received, which is $3.00 per share or $300 for one contract.
    - Breakeven Points:
        - Upper Breakeven = Short Call Strike + Net Premium Received = $110 + $3.00 = $113.00
        - Lower Breakeven = Short Put Strike - Net Premium Received = $90 - $3.00 = $87.00

1.2.2 Step-by-Step Guide to Executing an Iron Condor

- **Choosing the Right Underlying Asset:** You should choose an underlying instrument which has been trading in a clear range and avoid situations when you expect relevant changes / events which can have an impact on the volatility or the behavior / trend of the underlying instrument.
Example: Imagine you are looking at Stock XYZ, which has been trading in a relatively tight range between $95 and $105 for the past several weeks. The stock has low implied volatility, and there are no major news events expected soon.

- **Setting Up the Trade:**
    - **Delta:** Select strike prices for the call spread and the put spread that are outside the current trading range of the stock. For the bear call spread, choose a short call with a delta around 0.15 to 0.20 and a long call with a higher strike price. For the bull put spread, choose a short put with a delta around 0.15 to 0.20 and a long put with a lower strike price.
    Example: With XYZ trading at $100:
        - Bear call spread: Sell the $110 call (delta ~0.15), buy the $115 call.
        - Bull put spread: Sell the $90 put (delta ~0.15), buy the $85 put.

- **DTE (Days to Expiration):** Choose an expiration date that is typically 30 to 45 days out. This time frame strikes a balance between premium decay and time risk.
  Example: For Stock XYZ, you select options that expire in 35 days.

- **Executing the Trade:** Place an order to sell the iron condor, ensuring all four legs are included in one order to avoid legging risk.
  Example: You execute the iron condor trade:
    - Sell 1 $110 call, buy 1 $115 call, sell 1 $90 put, buy 1 $85 put.

1.2.3 Adjusting Iron Condors

Effective adjustment strategies are vital for managing iron condors, especially when the market moves against your position.

- **Rolling the Entire Iron Condor or One Side of the Iron Condor:** If the underlying asset starts moving towards one of your short strikes (either the call or the put side), you can "roll" the entre iron condor or only that side of the iron condor. Rolling involves closing the current spread and opening a new spread further out-of-the-money (OTM) and possibly further out in time. This will extend the range where the position is profitable and allows you to stay in the trade.
  Another option would be to roll up/down the unchallenged side of the iron condor collecting profits and additional premium. This can help you give additional buffer to the challenged side of the iron condor, but be aware that the overall range of your position will be reduced as a consequence, thus increasing the risk in case of volatility spikes.

  Case Study: Rolling the Spread (AAPL)

  Scenario: You have an iron condor on AAPL, with the stock trading at $150:

  - **Bear call spread:** Sold the $160 call, bought the $165 call.

- **Bull put spread:** Sold the $140 put, bought the $135 put.

If AAPL moves to $155, roll the entire spread up:

- **New call spread:** Sell the $165 call, buy the $170 call.
- **New put spread:** Sell the $145 put, buy the $140 put.

- **Converting the Position into an Iron Butterfly:** Converting an iron condor into an iron butterfly (described in the next paragraphs) is a strategy adjustment that traders can use to capitalize on a potential stabilization of the underlying asset's price near the center of the condor's range. The iron butterfly has a higher potential profit if the underlying asset price stays close to the strike price of the short options, but it also has a higher risk profile compared to an iron condor.

The iron butterfly is less forgiving than the iron condor, as it profits from a narrower price range.

Case Study: Converting to an Iron Butterfly (TSLA)

Scenario: Your iron condor on TSLA is set up with the stock at $600:

- **Bear call spread:** Sold the $620 call, bought the $625 call.
- **Bull put spread:** Sold the $580 put, bought the $575 put.

If TSLA approaches $620:

- **Close the put spread** to reduce risk.
- **Open a new put spread:** Sold the $620 put, bought the $615 put.
- **You now hold an iron butterfly:**
    - Bear call spread remains intact, with the sold $620 call and bought $625 call.
    - You keep the premium from the original put spread and the new one, reducing overall risk.

- The overall profitability range is now reduced because of the adjustment.

- **Closing the Iron Condor:** As already described in the previous chapters, closing the trade early can be a suitable option to lock in profits and reduce risk or to close the position to reduce losses in case the market outlook changed and it is no longer fitting with the position.

    Case Study: Closing the Trade Early (AMZN)

    Scenario: You have an iron condor on AMZN, trading at $3,200:

    - **Bear call spread:** Sold the $3,300 call, bought the $3,305 call.
    - **Bull put spread:** Sold the $3,100 put, bought the $3,095 put.

    If AMZN remains at $3,200 and 70% of the premium is collected:

    - Close the trade to lock in profits and reduce risk.
    - Execute orders to buy back the sold call and put, and sell the bought call and put

1.2.4 Estimating the Required Capital

The required capital for an iron condor is the maximum potential loss, which is the difference between the strikes of one spread, minus the net credit received.

Case Study: Capital Requirement (GOOGL)

Scenario: Iron condor on GOOGL, with the stock at $163:

- **Bear call spread:** Sold the $180 call, bought the $190 call.
- **Bull put spread:** Sold the $150 put, bought the $140 put.

Spread Width:

- Width of both call and put spreads = $10.

Net Credit Received:

- Total credit received from both spreads = $0.73.

Maximum Potential Loss:

- Maximum potential loss = $10 - $0.73 = $9.27 per share.

Required Capital:

- For 1 contract (100 shares), required capital = 100 * $9.27 = $927.

1.2.5 Conclusion

Iron condors are a powerful strategy for generating consistent income in a stable market. By understanding their structure, executing trades with precision, and managing risks through adjustments, traders can harness the benefits of this advanced options strategy.

UNLEASH THE POWER OF ADVANCED INCOME STRATEGIES

1.3 Iron Butterflies – A Precision Income Strategy

In the realm of options trading, butterflies represent a sophisticated strategy that offers a balance between risk and reward. Unlike more straightforward strategies such as covered calls or cash-secured puts, iron butterflies require a nuanced understanding of market behavior and precise execution. This chapter will guide you through the intricacies of iron butterfly spreads, providing clear examples and detailed explanations on how to set up, adjust, and manage these trades effectively. By the end of this chapter, you'll be equipped with the knowledge to use iron butterflies as a potent tool in your trading arsenal.

1.3.1 The Purpose of Iron Butterflies

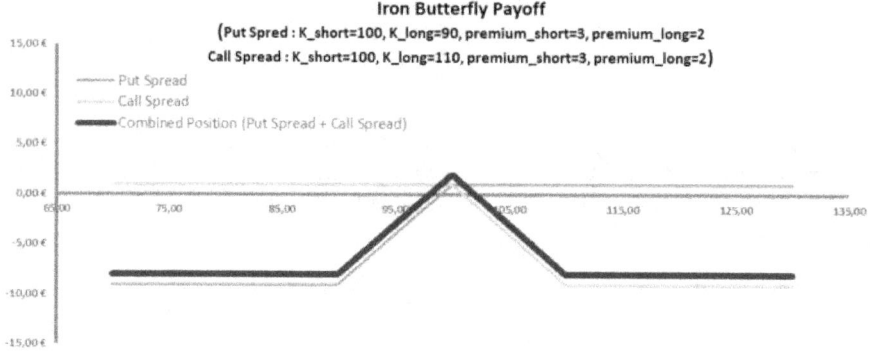

Figure 4 - Iron Butterfly Payoff

An iron butterfly spread is a neutral options strategy that combines bull and bear spreads with the same expiration date and three different strike prices. The strategy is designed to have a large profit zone around the middle strike price while limiting potential losses.

A standard iron butterfly spread consists of:

- **One Bull Spread:** This is the lower part of the butterfly.

- **One Bear Spread:** This is the upper part of the butterfly.

- **The short position of the bear spread and of the bull spread should have the same strike**

The maximum profit occurs if the underlying asset's price is at the middle strike price at expiration, and the maximum loss is limited to the initial cost of the spread.

Please be aware that you can also create butterflies with the same type of options (calls/puts):

- **One Long Call (or Put) at a Lower Strike Price:** This is the lower wing of the butterfly.

- **Two Short Calls (or Puts) at the Middle Strike Price:** This is the body of the butterfly.

- **One Long Call (or Put) at a Higher Strike Price:** This is the upper wing of the butterfly.

This kind of butterflies are different compared to the iron butterflies, especially regarding the capital requirement, cause they lead to a net cost when the trade is initiated and they can be slightly more difficult to adjust compared to the iron version.

Example: Constructing an Iron Butterfly Spread

Let's consider a practical example using a hypothetical stock, ABC Inc., currently trading at $100. You anticipate that ABC will trade close to $100 over the next month due to stable market conditions.

- **Selecting Strike Prices:** We choose the following strike prices for a call butterfly:
    - Buy 1 Put at $90 (Lower Strike)
    - Sell 1 Put at $100 (Middle Strike)
    - Sell 1 Call at $100 (Middle Strike)
    - Buy 1 Call at $110 (Upper Strike)

- **Calculating Premiums:** Assume the following premiums for each option:
    - Buy 1 Put at $90: $1.50 premium paid
    - Sell 1 Put at $100: $4.00 premium received
    - Sell 1 Call at $100: $8.00 premium received
    - Buy 1 Call at $110: $3.00 premium paid

- **Calculating Net Premium:** The net credit of the iron butterfly spread is calculated as:
    - Net Premium=

Premium Received from Middle Put and Call - (Premium Paid for Lower Put+Premium Paid for Upper Call)
- Net Premium=8.00+4.00-(1.50+3.00)=7,5

- **Determining Maximum Potential Loss:** The difference between the wing and body strikes minus the net premium received.
    - Maximum Potential Loss=(Difference between Strikes)–Net Premium
    - Maximum Potential Loss=(100 – 90) – 7.5 = 2.5

For one contract (100 shared), the maximum potential loss is: 100x2.50 = $250

- **Determining Maximum Profit and Breakeven Points:** The highest profit occurs if the stock is exactly at the middle strike price ($100) at expiration. The profit is the net initial credit.
    - Maximum Profit=Initial Credit, which is $7.5 per share or $750 for one contract
    - Breakeven Points:
        - Upper Breakeven = Short Call Strike + Net Premium Received = $100 + $7.50 = $117.50
        - Lower Breakeven = Short Put Strike – Net Premium Received = $100 - $7.50 = $92.50

1.3.2 Step-by-Step Guide to Executing an Iron Butterfly Spread

- **Choosing the Right Underlying Asset:** As described in the previous paragraph (Iron Condor) also for the Iron Butterfly the best underlying instrument should be the one trading in a clear range, without upcoming major events / earnings.
Example: Imagine you are looking at Stock XYZ, which has been trading around $100 with low volatility and no significant news expected.

- **Setting Up the Trade:**

- **Delta**: Select strike prices for the spreads that are centered around the current trading price of the stock.
  Choose a strike with a delta around 0.25 for the long options and a strike with a delta around 0.5 for short options.
  Example: With XYZ trading at $100:
    - Lower strike option: Buy the $95 put (delta ~0.25)
    - Middle strike options: Sell a $100 call and put (delta ~0.50 each)
    - Upper strike option: Buy the $105 call (delta ~0.25)
- **DTE (Days to Expiration)**: Choose an expiration date that is typically 30 to 45 days out to balance premium decay and time risk.
  Example: For Stock XYZ, you select options that expire in 35 days.

- **Executing the Trade**: Place an order to set up the iron butterfly spread, ensuring all four legs are included in one order to avoid legging risk.
  Example: You execute the iron butterfly spread trade:
    - Buy 1 $95 put, sell a $100 call and a $100 put, buy 1 $105 call.

1.3.3 Adjusting Butterflies

Effective adjustment strategies are crucial for managing iron butterfly spreads, especially when the market moves against your position.

- **Rolling the Iron Butterfly:** Rolling involves closing the current iron butterfly and opening a new one at different strike prices or with a different expiration date. There are several ways to roll:
    - **Rolling to a Different Expiration Date**: If the underlying asset is moving but you believe it will return to the range, you can roll the entire position to a later expiration date. This gives the underlying more time to move back to a favorable range.
    - **Rolling the Short Strikes**: If the underlying asset has moved in one direction, you can roll the short strikes closer to the current

price. This adjustment keeps the iron butterfly more centered around the new price.

Example: If you originally have an iron butterfly on SPY with short strikes at $440 and the stock moves to $450, you can roll your short strikes up to $450, creating a new iron butterfly centered around the current price.

- **Converting into an Iron Condor:** If the underlying price has moved close to one of the wings, you can convert the iron butterfly into an iron condor. This involves widening the spread to reduce the risk of a large loss.
  Close the losing short leg and buy back the closer wing. Sell a new short leg further out and buy a new wing to create an iron condor.
  Example: If the underlying asset has moved close to the upper short strike, you could close the upper short strike and the upper wing and sell a new call spread further up. This creates a wider range of profit, like an iron condor.

- **Moving One Wing:** If the underlying asset has moved away from the center, you can move just one wing of the iron butterfly to better capture potential profit. This creates an asymmetrical iron butterfly, which can be more forgiving if the underlying doesn't return to the center.
  Sell the closer wing and replace it with a new strike further away from the current price, increasing the distance between the short strike and the new wing.
  Example: If the stock price rises sharply, you can move the call wing higher while keeping the original put wing intact. This adjustment allows for continued profit potential if the stock price continues rising.

- **Adding Another Position (Double Butterfly):** If the underlying asset moves significantly away from your iron butterfly's center, you can add another iron butterfly around the new price. This adjustment is often called a "double butterfly" and can help you capitalize on a potential reversal.
  Open a new iron butterfly at a new strike price range around the current underlying price, while keeping the original position open.
  Example: If your original iron butterfly is centered at $100 and the underlying price moves to $110, you can open a new iron butterfly centered at $110, hoping for mean reversion.

- **Closing the Iron Butterfly:** Sometimes the best adjustment is to exit the position altogether, especially if the market is moving against you and no adjustment offers a favorable risk/reward profile.
  Early exiting the position can be also beneficial to capture profits and free up the capital for new trades.
  Example: If your original iron butterfly already earned more than 50% of the maximum potential profit in a short amount of time it could be beneficial to lock in the profits and move in with another trade.

1.3.4 Estimating the Required Capital

Estimating the required capital for iron butterfly spreads ensures you understand the risk and have adequate funds to cover potential losses.

Case Study: Capital Requirement (AMZN)

Scenario: Iron Butterfly on AMZN, with the stock at $165:

- Buy 1 $180 call, sell 1 $165 call and 1 $165 put, buy 1 $150 put

Spread Width:

- Width of both call spreads = $15.

Net Credit:

- Total cost of the spread = $9,27.

Maximum Potential Loss:

- Maximum potential loss = Spread Width - Net Credit = $5.73.

Required Capital:

- For 1 contract (100 shares), required capital = 100 * $5.73 = $573.

1.3.5 Conclusion

Iron Butterfly spreads are a powerful strategy for generating consistent income in a stable market. By understanding their structure, executing trades with precision, and managing risks through adjustments, traders can harness the benefits of this advanced options strategy.

1.4 RATIO SPREADS – BALANCING RISK AND REWARD

In the diverse world of options trading, ratio spreads stand out as a versatile strategy that can be tailored to suit various market conditions and trader preferences. This chapter will delve into the intricacies of ratio spreads, offering a step-by-step guide to executing these trades, detailed descriptions of trade setups, and insights into adjustments and capital requirements. By the end of this chapter, you'll understand how to effectively use ratio spreads to balance risk and reward in your trading portfolio.

1.4.1 The Purpose of Ratio Spreads

A ratio spread involves buying and selling different quantities of options with the same expiration date but different strike prices. Typically, it consists of buying one option and selling two or more options at a different strike price. This creates a directional bias, allowing traders to benefit from anticipated price movements while managing potential risks.

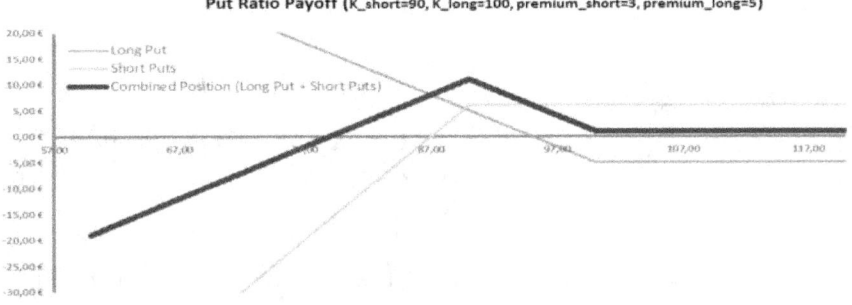

Figure 5 - Put Ratio Payoff

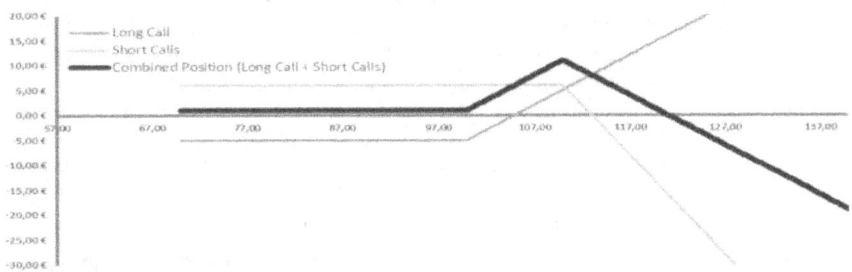

Figure 6 - Call Ratio Payoff

A standard structure of a ratio spread includes:

- **One Long Option:** This is the purchased option.
- **Multiple Short Options:** These are the sold options, usually with a higher strike price for calls or a lower strike price for puts.

The key characteristic of a ratio spread is the imbalance in the number of long and short options, creating a "ratio" between them. The most common ratio is 1:2, but traders can use other ratios depending on their market outlook and risk tolerance.

Example: Constructing a Call Ratio Spread

Let's consider a practical example using a hypothetical stock, XYZ Corp., currently trading at $50. You anticipate that XYZ will rise moderately over the next month but want to limit your risk exposure.

- **Selecting Strike Prices:** We choose the following strike prices for a call ratio spread:
    - Buy 1 Call at $50 (Lower Strike)
    - Sell 2 Calls at $55 (Higher Strike)
- **Calculating Premiums:** Assume the following premiums for each option:
    - Buy 1 Call at $50: $3.00 premium paid
    - Sell 2 Call at $55: $1.50 premium received (each)
- **Calculating Net Premium:** The net premium of the ratio spread is calculated as:
    - Net Premium=2×Premium Received from Higher Calls - (Premium Paid for Lower Call)
    - Net Premium=2×1.50-3.00=3.00−3.00=0

   In this case, the trade is executed at no cost, meaning you pay nothing to enter the position.

- **Determining Maximum Potential Loss:** The maximum loss is theoretically unlimited if the stock price rises significantly above the higher strike price, as the short calls create an obligation to sell the stock at the higher strike price.
    - Maximum Loss=Theoretically Unlimited
- **Determining Maximum Potential Profit and Breakeven Points:** The highest profit occurs if the stock is at the higher strike price

($55) at expiration. The profit is the difference between the higher strike price and the lower strike price, minus the net cost / plus the net premiums.

- Maximum Profit=(Higher Strike−Lower Strike)−Net Cost/+Net Premium = (55−50)−0=5
- Breakeven Points:
  - If Net Premium:
    - Breakeven=Short Call Strike + Maximum Profit + Net Credit = $55 + $5 + $0 = $60
  - If Net Cost:
    - Lower Breakeven Point=Long Call Strike + Net Cost
    - Upper Breakeven Point=Short Call Strike + Maximum Profit - Net Cost

1.4.2 Step-by-Step Guide to Executing a Ratio Spread

- **Choosing the Right Underlying Asset:** The underlying asset for a Ratio Spread should be stable / moderately bullish / bearish. Be careful in case of corporate events / earnings which can make the underlying asset spike in one direction or another.
  Example: Imagine you are looking at Stock ABC, which has been trading around $100 with moderate volatility and a bullish outlook.

- **Setting Up the Trade:**
  - **Delta:** Select strike prices for the call spread that reflect your market outlook.
    For the call ratio spread, choose a lower strike with a delta around 0.50 / 0.40 and higher strike calls with deltas around 0.30 / 0.2.
    Example: With ABC trading at $100:
    - Lower strike call: Buy the $100 call (delta ~0.50)
    - Higher strike calls: Sell two $110 calls (delta ~0.30 each)

- **DTE (Expiration Date):**
  - Choose an expiration date that is typically 30 to 45 days out to balance premium decay and time risk.

  Example: For Stock ABC, you select options that expire in 45 days

- **Executing the Trade:** Place an order to set up the ratio spread, ensuring all legs are included in one order to avoid legging risk.
  Example: You execute the ratio spread trade:
  - Buy 1 $100 call, sell 2 $110 calls.

1.4.3 Adjusting Ratio Spreads

Effective adjustment strategies are crucial for managing ratio spreads, especially when the market moves against your position.

- **Rolling the Short Options:** If the underlying asset is moving strongly towards the short strike(s) and the position is becoming risky, rolling can help reduce risk.
  Close the current short options and sell new ones at a further out-of-the-money (OTM) strike, ideally at the same expiration or further out.
  Example: You have a 1x2 call ratio spread with a long call at $100 and two short calls at $105. If the stock approaches $105 quickly, you can roll the short calls to $110 to reduce risk and give yourself more room.

- **Converting the Position into a Butterfly Spread:** If the underlying asset is near the short strike and you want to limit risk while still capitalizing on a potential profit zone.

  Buy an additional call or put at the same strike as your short options, converting the position into a butterfly spread.
  Example: With the same setup (long call at $100, two short calls at $105), you can buy a $110 call, creating a butterfly spread ($100/$105/$110). This caps both your risk and your profit potential, turning the position into a more controlled trade.

- **Converting the Position into a Vertical Spread:** If the underlying asset is moving significantly in the direction of the short options and you want to simplify the position while limiting risk.

Close one of the short options, converting the trade into a vertical spread.
Example: With a 1x2 call ratio spread (long $100, short two $105), you close one of the $105 calls, leaving you with a simple $100/$105 call vertical spread. This adjustment limits your downside risk.

- **Converting the Position into a Cash-Secured Put (only for Put Ratio Spreads):** If the underlying is moving towards the short strikes, you can decide to convert the position into a cash-secured put, while locking in the profits coming from the long and short option.
Close the existing long option and one of the short option and manage the remaining short option like a cash-secured put.
Example: If the stock is approaching your $100 strike (with a $105/$100 put ratio spread), you could close the long put and the one of the short put and keep the remaining short put, to be managed as a cash-secured put.

- **Doubling Down or Rolling into a Wider Ratio Spread:** If the underlying is slightly moving towards the short strikes, and you want to adjust for a more aggressive outlook.
Close the existing short options and open new ones at a wider spread, potentially increasing the number of short options.
Example: If the stock is approaching your $105 strike (with a $100/$105 ratio spread), you could roll the shorts to $110 or open a new 1x3 ratio spread (adding another short leg at $110).

- **Closing the Ratio Spread:** If the underlying asset moves strongly against the trade, and no adjustment provides a favorable risk/reward profile.
Close the entire position and reassess the market conditions.
Example: If your ratio spread has become too risky, with the underlying nearing the short strikes, exiting the position can prevent further losses.

1.4.4 Estimating Capital Requirements

Estimating the required capital for ratio spreads ensures you understand the risk and have adequate funds to cover potential losses.

For a put ratio spread, the capital requirement is affected by:

- Cost of the vertical spread: Short Put Premium – Long Put Premium
- Capital requirement for a cash-secured put

For a call ratio spread, the capital requirement is affected by:

- Cost of the vertical spread: Short Call Premium – Long Call Premium
- Capital requirement for a short call

Please be aware that the short call has unlimited risk and the capital requirement is affected by the broker risk management rules.

1.4.5 Conclusion

Ratio spreads are a powerful strategy for generating consistent income in a moderately moving market. By understanding their structure, executing trades with precision, and managing risks through adjustments, traders can harness the benefits of this advanced options strategy.

1.5 SHORT STRANGLES – PROFITING FROM STABILITY

In the landscape of options trading, the short strangle strategy stands out as a powerful tool for those looking to profit from market stability. This approach involves selling both a call and a put option with the same expiration date but different strike prices. The primary objective is to capitalize on the premiums received, anticipating that the underlying asset will remain within a certain price range. This chapter provides a comprehensive guide to understanding, executing, and managing short strangles, complete with real-life examples, detailed descriptions, and actionable insights. By the end of this chapter, you will be equipped with the knowledge to use short strangles effectively to generate income in relatively stable markets.

1.5.1 The Purpose of Short Strangles

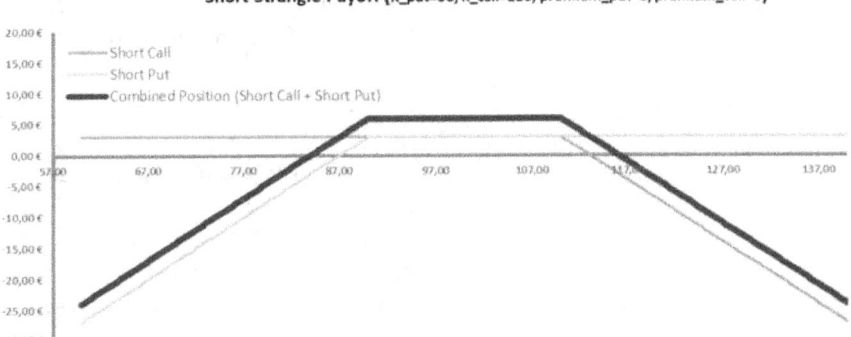

Figure 7 - Short Strangle Payoff

A short strangle is an options trading strategy that involves selling an out-of-the-money call and an out-of-the-money put simultaneously. The goal is to profit from the premiums received by betting that the underlying asset will not move significantly in either direction by the expiration date.

A standard structure of a strangle includes:

- **Short Call:** Selling an out-of-the-money call option.
- **Short Put:** Selling an out-of-the-money put option.

UNLEASH THE POWER OF ADVANCED INCOME STRATEGIES

The key characteristic of a short strangle is its potential to generate income through the decay of option premiums over time, provided the underlying asset remains within a specific range.

Example: Constructing a Short Strangle

Let's consider a practical example using a hypothetical stock, XYZ Corp., currently trading at $50. You anticipate that XYZ will trade within a narrow range over the next month.

- **Selecting Strike Prices:** We choose the following strike prices for a short strangle:
    - Sell 1 $55 Call (Out-of-the-Money Call)
    - Sell 1 $45 Put (Out-of-the-Money Put)

- **Calculating Premiums:** Assume the following premiums for each option:
    - Sell 1 $55 Call: $2.00 premium received
    - Sell 1 $45 Put: $2.50 premium received

- **Calculating Net Premium Received:** The net premium received from the strangle is calculated as:
    - Net Premium=(Premium Received for Call)+ (Premium Received for Put)
    - Net Premium=2.00+2.50=4.50

    In this case, the total premium received for entering the short strangle position is $4.50 per share, or $450 for one contract (100 shares).

- **Determining Maximum Potential Loss:** The maximum loss is theoretically unlimited if the stock price rises significantly above the higher strike price.
    - Maximum Loss=Theoretically Unlimited

- **Determining Maximum Potential Profit and Breakeven:** The highest profit occurs if the stock is between the upper ($55) and lower strike ($45) at expiration. The profit is the net premium received.
    - Maximum Profit=Net Premium=4.50
    - Breakeven Points:
        - Upper Breakeven Point=$55 (Call Strike Price) + $4.50 (Net Premium) = $59.50

- Lower Breakeven Point=$45 (Put Strike Price) - $4.50 (Net Premium) = $40.50

1.5.2 Step-by-Step Guide to Executing a Short Strangle

- **Choosing the Right Underlying Asset:** Like for the Iron Condors, also in this case the underlying asset should be stable and trading in a specific range, without corporate events / earnings due before the expiration of the positions.
  Example: Imagine you are looking at Stock ABC, which has been trading around $100 with relatively low volatility and no major news expected soon.

- **Setting Up the Trade:**
  - **Delta**: Select strike prices for the short strangle that are out-of-the-money and reflect a balance between risk and reward.
    For the short strangle, choose a call with a delta around 0.15 to 0.20 and a put with a delta around -0.15 to -0.20.
    Example: With ABC trading at $100:
    - Sell 1 $110 call (delta ~0.15)
    - Sell 1 $90 put (delta ~-0.15)
  - **DTE (Days to Expiration)**: Choose an expiration date that aligns with the anticipated period of stability, typically 30 to 45 days out.
    Example: For Stock ABC, you select options that expire in 45 days.

- **Executing the Trade**: Place an order to set up the short strangle, ensuring both legs are included in one order to avoid legging risk.
  Example: You execute the short strangle trade:
  - Sell 1 $110 call, sell 1 $90 put.

1.5.3 Adjusting Short Strangles

Effective adjustment strategies are crucial for managing short strangles, especially when the market moves against your position or volatility increases unexpectedly.

- **Rolling the Strangle / One Side of the Strangle:** Rolling involves closing your current strangle position and opening a new one with different strike prices or a different expiration date. Rolling can be done in several ways:
    - **Rolling Out**: Extending the time horizon by closing the current strangle and opening a new one with the same strikes but a later expiration date. This gives the trade more time to work out and allows time decay (theta) to erode the option premiums further.
    - **Rolling Up or Down**: Moving the strike prices further out-of-the-money (OTM) to reduce the likelihood of the options being in the money (ITM). For example, if the underlying asset moves toward the call strike, you could roll the entire strangle up by selecting higher strikes for both the call and put. You can also choose to roll up the unchallenged side while keeping the challenged side in place without any modification. Sometimes, it can be effective to adjust only the leg of the strangle that is being challenged, rather than the entire position. You should carefully assess the situation and the adjustment costs to identify the best solution (keep into consideration that, as already discussed in the Iron Condor chapter, rolling only one side will reduce the profitability range).

  Example: Suppose you sold a strangle on XYZ stock with a $50 call and a $40 put, and the stock rises to $48. You might roll the strangle to a $55 call and a $45 put, extending the expiration date by another month. This adjustment maintains the position while reducing the risk of the call option being ITM.

- **Converting One Side into a Vertical Spread:** Converting to a Vertical Spread involves adding a position that offsets some of the risk associated with the original strangle. This can involve buying options to cover the potential loss.

  If the underlying asset moves sharply in one direction, you can buy a call or put option at a strike price closer to the current market price to limit the potential loss. This will convert one side of the strangle into a vertical credit spread.

Example: If you sold a strangle with a $50 call and a $40 put, and the stock rises to $48, you could buy a $48 call to cap your potential losses on the call side.

- **Converting the Position into an Iron Condor:** If the market moves toward one of your strikes, you can convert the strangle into an iron condor. This adjustment simply extends the previous adjustment (converting one side into a vertical spread) and involves adding a credit spread on the opposite side of the strangle, creating a defined risk strategy.
Example: Suppose you sold a $50/$40 strangle on XYZ stock, and the stock rises to $48. You could convert the position into an iron condor by buying a protective put (for example with a $38 strike) and call (for example with a $52 strike) if you are worried about potential spikes in both directions. This creates a defined risk position, and it can be then managed like an iron condor.

- **Converting the Position into an Inverted Strangle:** One effective method for adjusting a short strangle when the market moves against you is to convert it into an inverted strangle. This involves repositioning your strikes such that the new call strike is lower than the new put strike, effectively "inverting" the position. This adjustment helps in managing losses and potentially turning an adverse situation into a profitable one. Let's delve into the specifics of this method with detailed examples and step-by-step instructions.

An inverted strangle involves selling a call and a put with the call strike price lower than the put strike price. This is the opposite of a typical strangle, where the call strike is higher than the put strike. This inversion creates a position that benefits from a significant movement in the underlying asset, regardless of direction.

Step-by-Step Guide to Converting to an Inverted Strangle:

- **Assess the Initial Position***:* Let's start with a short strangle position.
  Example:
    - Underlying Stock: XYZ
    - Current Price: $100
    - Original Position: Sold 110 Call for $2 and Sold 90 Put for $2
    - Expiration: 30 days
- **Monitor the Market Movement***:* Assume the stock price of XYZ rises significantly to $115. This move puts the 110 Call deep in-the-money (ITM), resulting in potential

losses. The 90 Put, on the other hand, is now far out-of-the-money (OTM) and has minimal value.
- **Decide to Adjust**: Given the significant rise in the stock price, the next step is to adjust the position to manage the risk and potential losses from the ITM call. Converting to an inverted strangle can help in this scenario.
- **Close the Original Position**: To initiate the adjustment, close the original short strangle position by buying back the ITM call and the OTM put. You can also choose to start moving only the OTM one (this will lock in profits), by progressively moving it closer to the other option till the final inversion.
  Example:
  - Buy to close the 110 Call for $7 (realizing a loss of $5 per share, or $500 per contract).
  - Buy to close the 90 Put for $0.10 (realizing a gain of $1.90 per share, or $190 per contract).
- **Establish the Inverted Strangle**: Next, establish the inverted strangle by selling a new call option with a strike price below the current stock price and selling a new put option with a strike price above the current stock price.

  Example:
  - Sell to open the 105 Call for $5 (new call strike below current stock price of $115).
  - Sell to open the 120 Put for $5 (new put strike above current stock price of $115).

  The new position:
  - Short 105 Call
  - Short 120 Put
- **Calculate the Net Credit:** To understand the overall impact of the adjustment, calculate the net credit received from the original and new positions.
  - Original Position Credit:

- 110 Call: $2
 - 90 Put: $2
 - Total: $4
- Adjustment Transactions:
  - Buy back 110 Call: -$7
  - Buy back 90 Put: -$0.10
  - Sell 105 Call: $5
  - Sell 120 Put: $5
- Net Credit from Adjustment:
  - (-$7) + (-$0.10) + $5 + $5 = $2.90
- Total Net Credit:
  - $4 (original) + $2.90 (adjustment) = $6.90

The total net credit received from the entire sequence of trades is $6.90 per share, or $690 per contract.

- **Monitor and Manage the New Position:** Once the inverted strangle is in place, continue to monitor the underlying stock's price and the options' Greeks. The key is to actively manage the position, making further adjustments if necessary to stay within your risk tolerance.
- **Closing the Strangle:** In some cases, the best adjustment is to close the position entirely. This is especially true if the market has moved significantly against you, if you're nearing expiration with little chance of recovery or if you already gained most of the maximum potential profit in a short amount of time.

If the market has moved sharply against your strangle and the potential losses exceed your risk tolerance, closing the position to cut losses could be an option.

Example: If XYZ stock rises to $55 and you sold a $50/$40 strangle, the call will be at a loss. Rather than rolling or adjusting, you might decide to close the entire position to prevent further losses.

1.5.4 Estimating Capital Requirements

Estimating the required capital for short strangles ensures you understand the risk and have adequate funds to cover potential losses.

Since the short strangle is a not defined risk strategy, the capital required to hold it is primarily determined by the requirements set by your broker. For a short strangle, the capital requirement is typically based on the worst-case scenario, which considers the maximum potential loss if the underlying asset moves significantly in either direction.

Generally, the capital requirement is computed by considering:

- The capital requirement for a short put option
- The capital requirement for a short call option
- A combination of both, depending on the risk management rules applied by the broker

1.5.5 Conclusion

Short strangles offer a powerful means of generating income through options trading, especially in stable markets. By understanding the structure, benefits, risks, and effective adjustment strategies, traders can harness the potential of short strangles to achieve consistent profits. This chapter has provided a detailed, step-by-step guide to executing, managing, and adjusting short strangles, complete with real-life examples and practical insights. With this knowledge, you are well-equipped to incorporate short strangles into your options trading toolkit, enhancing your ability to profit from market stability while managing risks effectively.

1.6 SHORT STRADDLES – PROFITING FROM STABILITY

In this chapter, we will explore the intricacies of the short straddle strategy, an advanced options trading technique that can be highly profitable for those who understand its mechanics and risks. A short straddle involves selling both a call and a put option with the same strike price and expiration date. This strategy profits from low volatility in the underlying asset, as the premium collected from selling the options can lead to significant gains if the stock price remains relatively stable.

By the end of this chapter, you will have a comprehensive understanding of how to execute a short straddle, set up the trade with appropriate deltas and days to expiration (DTE), manage and adjust the position, and estimate the required capital. We will also provide real-world examples to illustrate these concepts in practice.

1.6.1 The Purpose of Short Straddles

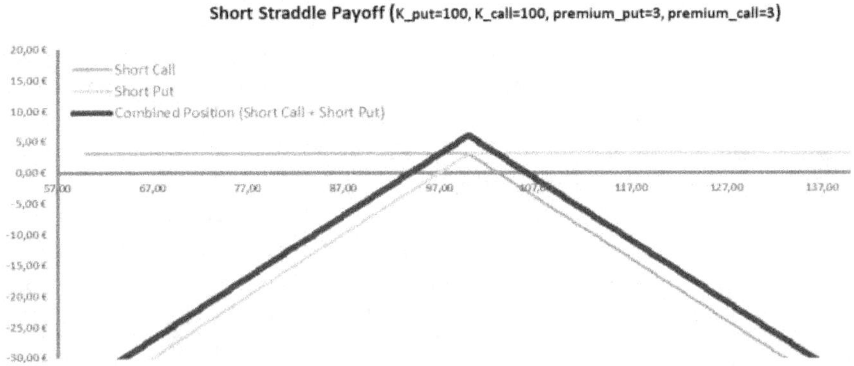

Figure 8 - Short Straddle Payoff

A short straddle is an options strategy that involves selling one call and one put option at the same strike price and expiration date on the same underlying asset. The primary goal of this strategy is to profit from the premiums collected from selling these options, betting that the underlying asset will not experience significant price movement before the options expire.

A standard structure of a straddle includes:

- **Short Call:** Selling a call option.

- **Short Put:** Selling a put option.

- The call and the put should have the same strike (usually at the money)

The Key characteristic of a short strangle is its potential to generate income through the decay of option premiums over time, provided that the underlying asset remains within a specific range.

1.6.2 Step-by-Step Guide to Executing a Short Straddle

Let's walk through the process of setting up a short straddle trade, from selecting the underlying asset to managing the position.

- **Choosing the Right Underlying Asset:** Choosing the right underlying asset is crucial for a successful short straddle. Ideally, you want to select an asset that is expected to have low volatility and minimal price movement during the life of the options. Stocks with stable price histories or that are in a consolidation phase are good candidates.
  Example: Suppose you choose XYZ Corp., a stock that has been trading in a tight range between $95 and $105 for the past several months and currently trades at $100.

- **Setting Up the Trade:**
  - **Delta:** For a short straddle, you sell both a call and a put option at the same strike price, which is typically close to the current trading price of the underlying asset.
    Example: With XYZ Corp. trading at $100, you decide to sell a $100 call and a $100 put.
  - **DTE (Days to Expiration):** The expiration date determines the time frame in which the underlying asset must remain relatively stable. Generally, short straddles are set up with 30 to 45 days to expiration (DTE), balancing the premium collected with the risk exposure.
    Example: You choose options with 30 days to expiration.

- **Executing the Trade:** you execute the trade by selling both the call and put options.
  Example: You execute the short straddle trade:
  - Sell 1 XYZ $100 Call for $4.00

- Sell 1 XYZ $100 Put for $4.00

1.6.3 Adjusting Short Straddles

Managing a short straddle requires vigilance and a proactive approach to mitigate risks and maximize profits. Given the unlimited risk on both sides of the trade, traders must be prepared to adjust as the underlying asset's price moves. Here, we will explore several adjustment strategies that can help manage a short straddle position.

Most of the adjustment techniques were already described in the previous chapter (Short Strangles) due to the similar nature of the two strategies. They will be anyway reported here for sake of completeness.

- **Rolling Out the Straddle / Rolling Up or Down One Side of the Straddle:** Rolling involves closing your current straddle position and opening a new one with different strike prices or a different expiration date. Rolling can be done in several ways:
    - **Rolling Out**: Extending the time horizon by closing the current strangle and opening a new one with the same strikes but a later expiration date. This gives the trade more time to work out and allows time decay (theta) to erode the option premiums further.
    - **Rolling Up or Down**: Moving the strike prices further out-of-the-money (OTM) to reduce the likelihood of the options being in the money (ITM). For example, if the underlying asset challenges the call strike, you could roll the entire straddle up by selecting higher strike for both the call and put. You can also choose to roll up the unchallenged side while keeping the challenged side in place without any modification (see inverted strangle). Sometimes, it can be effective to adjust only the leg of the straddle that is being challenged, rather than the entire position. You should carefully assess the situation and the adjustment costs to identify the best

solution (keep into consideration that, as already discussed in the Iron Condor chapter, rolling only one side will reduce the profitability range).

Example: Suppose you sold a straddle on XYZ stock with a $50 call and put, and the stock rises to $55. You might roll the strangle to a $55 call and put, extending the expiration date by another month. This adjustment maintains the position while reducing the risk of the call option being ITM.

- **Converting One Side into a Vertical Spread:** Converting to a Vertical Spread involves adding a position that offsets some of the risk associated with the original strangle. This can involve buying options to cover the potential loss.

  If the underlying asset moves sharply in one direction, you can buy a call or put option at a strike price closer to the current market price to limit the potential loss. This will convert one side of the straddle into a vertical credit spread.

  Example: If you sold a straddle with a $50 call and put, and the stock rises to $53, you could buy a $55 call to cap your potential losses on the call side.

- **Converting the Position into an Iron Condor:** If the market moves away from your strike, you can convert the straddle into an iron condor. This adjustment simply extends the previous adjustment (converting one side into a vertical spread) and involves adding a credit spread on the opposite side of the straddle, creating a defined risk strategy.

  Example: Suppose you sold a $50 strangle on XYZ stock, and the stock rises to $54. You could convert the position into an iron condor by selling a put spread, such as selling the $45 put and buying the $40 put. This creates a defined risk position, reducing potential losses on the put side.

- **Converting the Position into a Strangle / Inverted Strangle:** If the underlying asset's price starts moving significantly, converting the straddle into a strangle / inverted strangle by adjusting the strike prices can help manage delta and gamma risk.

  Example: If ABC's stock price moves from $150 to $160, you can adjust by moving the put option's strike price closer to the current stock price.
  - **Initial Trade:**
    - Sell 1 ABC $150 Call for $7.00
    - Sell 1 ABC $150 Put for $7.00
  - **Adjustment:**

- Buy back the ABC $150 Put for $2.00 (gain of $5.00)
- Sell a new ABC $160 Put for $6.00

This adjustment converts the position into a short strangle with $150 Call and $160 Put, maintaining a neutral stance with adjusted strike prices.

- **Closing the Straddle:** In some cases, the best adjustment is to close the position entirely. This is especially true if the market has moved significantly against you, if you're nearing expiration with little chance of recovery or if you already gained most of the maximum potential profit in a short amount of time.
  If the market has moved sharply against your straddle and the potential losses exceed your risk tolerance, closing the position to cut losses could be an option.
  Example: If XYZ stock rises to $55 and you sold a $50 straddle, the call will be at a loss. Rather than rolling or adjusting, you might decide to close the entire position to prevent further losses.

1.6.4 Estimating the Required Capital

Capital requirements for a short straddle depend on the margin requirements set by your broker and the potential risk of the position. Brokers typically require a margin to cover potential losses, which can vary based on the underlying asset's price, volatility, and the strike prices of the options sold.

Example:

- Underlying Stock: XYZ Corp.
- Stock Price: $100
- Margin Requirement: Typically, brokers might require a percentage of the underlying stock price plus the premium received.
- Assume a margin requirement of 20% of the stock price plus the premium received.

Margin Calculation:

- 20% of $100 = $20

- Premium Received = $8
- Total Margin Required per Contract = $20 + $8 = $28 per share
- For 1 Contract (100 shares): $28 * 100 = $2,800

This margin covers the potential risk of significant moves in the underlying asset.

1.6.5 Conclusion

The short straddle is a powerful options strategy that can generate substantial profits in a low-volatility environment. However, it requires careful monitoring and adjustments to manage the unlimited risk on both sides of the trade. By understanding the mechanics of the strategy, setting up the trade with appropriate delta and DTE, and employing effective adjustments, traders can effectively utilize short straddles.

UNLEASH THE POWER OF ADVANCED INCOME STRATEGIES

1.7 Collar - A Balanced Approach to Risk Management

In the world of options trading, managing risk while seeking profit can often feel like walking a tightrope. For traders seeking to protect gains or limit potential losses, the collar strategy offers a balanced approach that marries the benefits of both covered calls and protective puts. This chapter delves deeply into the collar strategy, offering a comprehensive guide to executing, setting up, adjusting, and estimating capital requirements.

1.7.1 The Purpose of Collars

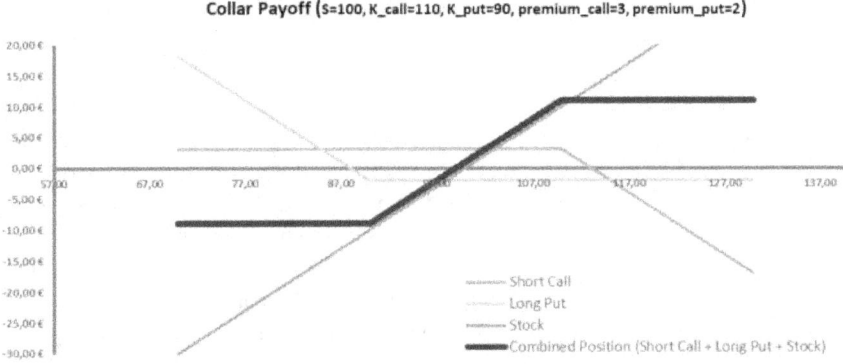

Figure 9 - Collar Payoff

The Collar Strategy involves holding a long position in an underlying stock while simultaneously buying a protective put option and selling a call option. This strategy creates a "collar" around the stock's price, effectively limiting potential losses and capping potential gains. It is particularly useful for investors who want to lock in profits while managing the risk of price declines.

A standard structure of a collar includes:

- **Long Stock Position**: Ownership of the underlying asset.

- **Protective Put**: An option purchased to hedge against a decline in the stock's price.

- **Covered Call**: An option sold to generate income, which caps the potential upside of the stock.

UNLEASH THE POWER OF ADVANCED INCOME STRATEGIES

1.7.2 Step-by-Step Guide to Executing a Collar Trade

To illustrate the collar strategy, let's walk through a detailed example with a fictional stock, XYZ Corp.

- **Choosing the Right Underlying Asset:** Before initiating the collar strategy, you need to assess the underlying stock. Let's assume XYZ Corp. is currently trading at $100, and you believe it will remain stable or have modest movement in the near term.
- **Setting Up the Trade:**
    - **Delta**: For the protective put (it protects against significant downside risk) you should choose a strike price that offers sufficient protection, but does not require an excessive premium. Usually, delta might be around -0.30.
    Example: In our example, you might select a put with a strike price of $90, which gives you a $10 cushion against potential declines. For the covered call (it generates income, but caps the upside potential), you should select a strike price above the current stock price to benefit from potential gains while collecting premium income. Usually, delta might be around 0.30.
    Example: For XYZ Corp., you might choose a strike price of $110.
    - **DTE (Days to Expiration)**: Select an expiration date that aligns with your investment horizon. Shorter DTE options generally have less premium and less time for the underlying price to move.
    Example: For this example, a 30-day expiration might be appropriate.
- **Execute the Trade:** You execute the trade by buying the put and the stock and selling the call.
    Example:
    - Buy 1 XYZ $90 Put for $1.50.
    - Sell 1 XYZ $110 Call for $2.00.
    - Buy 100 shares of XYZ Corp for $10000.00.

1.7.3 Adjusting the Collar

While collars provide a protective structure, market movements or shifts in strategy may necessitate adjustments to the original position. Adjustments are necessary when the underlying stock moves significantly or when the market outlook changes. Here's how to handle common scenarios:

- **Rolling the Collar:** Rolling the collar is always a viable option in case you want to give additional time to your strategy.
  To do so, you should close the existing options and open a new call and put with later expiration date.

- **Rolling the Call Option:** Rolling the call option involves closing out the existing short call position and opening a new one at a different strike price or expiration date. This adjustment is often used when the stock price is approaching or has exceeded the strike price of the short call.
    - **Rolling Up**: If the stock rises, you may want to roll up the call to capture more potential upside.
      Example: Suppose you own 100 shares of XYZ stock, currently trading at $95, and have sold a $100 call while buying an $85 put. If XYZ rises to $98, you may want to roll up the call (buy back the $100 Call, sell a new $105 Call) to capture more potential upside.
    - **Rolling Down**: if the stock drops, the call option becomes less valuable, and you may want to roll down the call to collect more premium.
      Example: If XYZ drops to $88, the call option becomes less valuable, and you may want to roll down the call to collect more premium (buy back the $100 Call, sell a new $95 Call)

- **Early Closing:** As described in the previous chapters, early closing the trade can be a viable option to cut the losses or to lock in the profits when you are satisfied with them (i.e.. the strategy worked out well in a short period of time, capturing most of the potential profits).
  In those situations, you can close the positions to free up capital for other strategies / positions.

- **Converting to a Synthetic Covered Call:** If the stock price rises significantly and the put option becomes nearly worthless, you might consider converting the collar into a synthetic covered call by removing the put.

Example: If XYZ rises from $95 to $105, the $85 put may have very little value. You could sell the $85 Put (removing downside protection) and keep the $100 Call. Now, you have a position like a covered call, where the primary risk is downside exposure to the stock, but you still collect premium from the call option.

1.7.4 Estimating Capital Requirements

To estimate the capital required for a collar strategy, consider the following components:

- **Stock Purchase**

- **Long Put (Premium Paid)**

- **Short Call (Premium Received)**

The total capital requirement should cover the cost of acquiring 100 shares of the underlying asset and it can be reduced / increase by the net premium / cost (put and call).

Example

- The cost of buying the put option (XYZ $90 Put): $1.50 per share × 100 shares = $150.

- The income generated from selling the call option (XYZ $110 Call): $2.00 per share × 100 shares = $200.

- Stock Purchase: 100 x $100 = $10000.

- Net Capital Required: Cost of Protective Put – Premium Collected from Covered Call + Stock Purchase: $150 - $200 + $10000 = $9950

1.7.5 Conclusion

The collar strategy is a powerful tool for managing risk while still participating in potential gains. By carefully selecting the right put and call options, and adjusting as the market changes, traders can effectively hedge their stock positions. With a clear understanding of trade setup, delta and DTE considerations, adjustment strategies, and capital requirements, you can use the collar to protect your investments and achieve a balanced approach to risk management.

CHAPTER 2

THE ULTIMATE CHEAT SHEET: COMPARING TOP OPTION INCOME STRATEGIES

This summary table provides a detailed comparison of various option income strategies, highlighting their components, effects on theta and volatility, and the optimal market conditions for their use. It serves as a quick reference guide, helping you to identify the best strategy for your trading objectives and understand the capital requirements and potential adjustments needed for each approach.

2.1 SUMMARY CHEAT SHEET

This table provides a clear overview of various option income strategies, their components, effects, ideal conditions, and best practices for adjustments. Each strategy is unique, and understanding these nuances will help you choose the right one based on your trading goals and market conditions.

- **Strategy:** The name of the option income strategy being summarized, such as Covered Call, Cash-Secured Put, Iron Condor, etc.

- **Components:** This column lists the specific options positions involved in the strategy. Components include long or short calls and puts, and whether they are combined with stock positions.

- **Theta Effect:** Theta measures the rate at which an option's value decreases as it approaches expiration, with a positive effect meaning the strategy benefits from time decay.

- **Volatility Effect:** This column describes how the strategy's profitability is affected by changes in market volatility.

- **Market Condition:** The ideal market conditions for implementing the strategy, such as trending, range-bound, high volatility, or low volatility markets.

- **Risk:** Describes whether the strategy has defined risk (known maximum loss) or undefined risk (potential for unlimited loss).

- **Best DTE (Days to Expiration):** The optimal number of days until the options expire for the strategy to be most effective.

- **Best Delta of Single Components:** The ideal delta for the individual options in the strategy, which influences the sensitivity of the strategy's price to changes in the underlying asset's price.

- **Adjustment Methods:** Methods to manage or adjust the position if market conditions change or if the trade moves against you.

- **Capital Requirement:** The formula or method used to calculate the capital required to execute the strategy. This may include the cost of options, margin requirements, or collateral.

UNLEASH THE POWER OF ADVANCED INCOME STRATEGIES

Strategy	Components	Theta Effect	Volatility Effect	Market Condition	Risk	Best DTE	Best Delta	Adjustment Methods	Capital Requirement
Covered Call	Long Stock, Short Call	Positive	Decrease preferred	Neutral to slightly bullish	Undefined	30-60	Call: 0.20-0.40	Rolling the Covered Call, Converting the Position into a Collar, Closing the Covered Call	Stock price * 100 – (Premium received)
Cash-Secured Put	Short Put, Cash	Positive	Decrease preferred	Neutral to slightly bullish	Undefined	30-60	Put: 0.20-0.40	Rolling the Put Option, Converting the Position into a Credit Spread, Converting the Position into a Strangle / Straddle, Closing the Cash-Secured Put	Strike price * 100 – (Premium received)
Put Credit Spread	Short Put, Long Put	Positive	Decrease preferred	Neutral to slightly bullish	Defined	30-45	Short Put: 0.30-0.40, Long Put: 0.10-0.15	Rolling the Spread, Converting the Position into Iron Condor / Butterfly, Selling an Additional Call or Put, Selling an Out-of-the-Money Call or Put, Closing the Spread	Difference in strike prices * 100 – (Premium received)
Call Credit Spread	Short Call, Long Call	Positive	Decrease preferred	Neutral to slightly bearish	Defined	30-45	Short Call: 0.30-0.40, Long Call: 0.10-0.15	Rolling the Spread, Converting the Position into Iron Condor / Butterfly, Selling an Additional Call or Put, Selling an Out-of-the-Money Call or Put, Closing the Spread	Difference in strike prices * 100 – (Premium received)
Iron Condor	Short Put, Short Call, Long Call	Positive	Decrease preferred	Range-bound	Defined	30-45, 0-30	Short Put/Call: 0.20-0.30, Long Put/Call: 0.05-0.10	Rolling the Iron Condor or One Side of the Iron Condor, Converting the Position into an Iron Butterfly, Closing the Iron Condor	Max(Difference in put strikes * 100, Difference in call strikes * 100)
Iron Butterfly	Short Call, Long Call, Short Put, Long Put	Positive	Decrease preferred	Range-bound	Defined	30-45	Short Put/Call: 0.50, Long Put/Call: 0.20-0.30	Rolling the Iron Butterfly, Converting into an Iron Condor, Moving One Wing, Adding Another Position (Double Butterfly), Closing the Short Options	Max(Difference in wings' put strikes * 100, Difference in wings' call strikes * 100)
Put Ratio Spread	Long Put, 2 Short Puts	Positive	Decrease preferred	Mildly bearish	Undefined	30-45	Long Put: 0.20-0.30, Short Puts: 0.40-0.50	Rolling the Short Options, Converting the Position into a Butterfly Spread, Converting the Position into a Vertical Spread, Converting the Position into a Cash-Secured Put (only for Put Ratio Spreads), Doubling Down or Rolling into a Wider Ratio Spread, Closing the Ratio Spread	Max(Difference in strike prices * 100, Short strike price * 100)
Call Ratio Spread	Long Call, 2 Short Calls	Positive	Decrease preferred	Mildly bullish	Undefined	30-45	Long Call: 0.20-0.30, Short Calls: 0.40-0.50	Rolling the Short Options, Converting the Position into a Butterfly Spread, Converting the Position into a Vertical Spread, Converting the Position into a Cash-Secured Put (only for Put Ratio Spreads), Doubling Down or Rolling into a Wider Ratio Spread, Closing the Ratio Spread	Max(Difference in strike prices * 100, Short Call Margin Requirement based on broker rules)

Table 1 - Cheat Sheet - Option Income Strategies

UNLEASH THE POWER OF ADVANCED INCOME STRATEGIES

Strategy	Components	Theta Effect	Volatility Effect	Market Condition	Risk	Best DTE	Best Delta	Adjustment Methods	Capital Requirement
Short Strangle	Short Put, Short Call	Positive	Decrease preferred	Range-bound	Undefined	30-45	Put/Call: 0.15-0.20	Rolling the Strangle / One Side of the Strangle; Converting One Side into a Vertical Spread; Converting the Position into an Iron Condor; Converting the Position into an Inverted Strangle; Closing the Strangle	Margin requirement based on broker rules
Short Straddle	Short Put, Short Call	Positive	Decrease preferred	Range-bound	Undefined	30-45	Put/Call: 0.50	Rolling Out the Straddle / Rolling Up or Down One Side of the Straddle; Converting One Side into a Vertical Spread; Converting the Position into an Iron Condor; Converting the Position into a Strangle / Inverted Strangle; Closing the Straddle	Margin requirement based on broker rules
Collar	Long Stock, Short Call, Long Put	Negative (slightly)	Decrease preferred	Neutral to slightly bullish	Defined	30-45	Call: 0.30; Put: 0.20-0.30	Rolling the Collar; Rolling the Call Option; Closing the Collar	Stock price * 100 shares + cost of the put – (Premium received)

CHAPTER 3

STOCK REPAIR STRATEGY

In the world of options trading, encountering a losing position is an inevitable part of the game. Even the most seasoned traders face trades that go against them, and it's essential to have strategies in place to manage and recover from such situations. One such strategy is the Stock Repair Strategy, a technique designed to help traders recover from a losing stock position while limiting further risk. In this chapter, we will explore the Stock Repair Strategy in depth, providing a step-by-step guide, real examples, and detailed explanations of trade setup, adjustments, and capital estimation.

3.1 THE PURPOSE OF THE STOCK REPAIR STRATEGY

The Stock Repair Strategy aims to assist traders in mitigating losses on a stock position that has declined in value. The strategy works by using options to potentially repair the position and offset some of the losses, effectively making the recovery process more manageable. It's particularly useful when the trader still believes in the underlying stock's long-term prospects but needs a way to handle the immediate downside.

The Stock Repair Strategy typically involves using a combination of options—specifically, a covered call and a long call spread—to repair a losing stock position. The core idea is to limit the losses on the stock and potentially profit from a rebound while managing risk using options.

A standard structure of a stock repair strategy includes:

- **Covered Call**: Involves selling a call option against a long stock position to collect premium income.

- **Long Call Spread**: Involves buying a call option (usually at the money) and simultaneously selling a higher strike call option (usually with the same strike as the covered call) to limit risk and potentially benefit from upward price movements.

- The increment between the strike prices (long call vs short calls) should be approximately half of the overall loss. Ideally, the OTM calls sold would have a premium of about half the price of the purchased ATM options. Therefore, the overall position should have an overall cost next to nothing. The trader can also evaluate using longer dated options to produce a net credit.

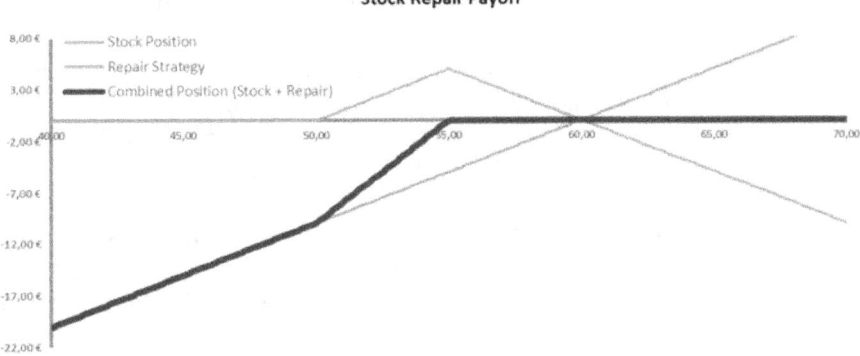

Figure 10 - Stock Repair Payoff

The strategy aims to recover most / all the loss by reducing the breakeven point. The expectation is that the stock will rebound before the strategy expiration to trigger the repairment mechanism.

Example: Constructing a Stock Repair Strategy

Assume you own 100 shares of XYZ Corporation, which you purchased at $60 per share. Due to a market downturn, XYZ has fallen to $50 per share, resulting in an unrealized loss of $1,000. You believe XYZ has long-term potential but need to manage your current position.

- **Selecting Strike Prices:** We choose the following strike prices for the stock repair strategy:
    - Buy $50 Call (At-the-Money Call)
    - Sell 2 $55 Calls (Out-of-the-Money Calls)

- **Calculating Premiums:** Assume the following premiums for each option:

UNLEASH THE POWER OF ADVANCED INCOME STRATEGIES

- Buy 1 $50 Call: $2.00 premium paid
- Sell 2 $55 Calls: $1.00 x 2 = $2.00 premium received

- **Calculating Net Premium / Cost Received:** The net premium received from the strategy is calculated as:
  - Net Premium/Cost=(Premium Received for Calls)-(Premium Paid for Call)
  - Net Premium/Cost=2.00-2.00=0.00

  With the mentioned setup the stock repair strategy does not have any cost. Please be aware that it is not always the case and it is absolutely possible that the premiums received from the short calls cannot completely cover the cost of the long option.

- **Determining Maximum Potential Loss:** The maximum loss is theoretically reached in case the stock falls to 0.
  - Maximum Loss=Current Stock Price x 100 shared

- **Determining Maximum Potential Profit and Breakeven:** The highest profit occurs if the stock reaches or goes beyond the strike of the upper calls ($55) at expiration. The profit is the sum of the price appreciation and the difference between the call strikes and the original net premium / cost.
  - Maximum Profit=Stock Appreciation + Difference between the Strikes + Net Premium / - Net Cost = ($55-$50) + ($55-$50) +$0 = $10
  - Breakeven Points (overall strategy):
    - Breakeven Point=$55
      - Stock (if the Stock reaches $55): $60 - $55 = - $5
      - Repair Strategy (if the Stock reaches $55): $5
      - Total Profit / Loss (if the Stock reaches $55): $0

3.2 STEP-BY-STEP GUIDE TO EXECUTING THE STOCK REPAIR STRATEGY

Let's delve into the previous example to illustrate how the Stock Repair Strategy is executed.

UNLEASH THE POWER OF ADVANCED INCOME STRATEGIES

- **Choosing the Right Underlying Asset:** To initiate a stock repair strategy you should have experienced a relevant loss on an already owned stock. In the previous example, the trader owned 100 shares of XYZ Corporation purchased at $60 per share. Due to a market downturn, the stock XYZ has fallen to $50, and the trader experienced an unrealized loss of $1,000. It is useful to execute the stock repair strategy fi the trader believe that the stock can rebound.

- **Setting Up the Trade:**
    - **Delta**: The first component of the repair strategy is to sell a call option against the stock you own. This generates premium income and helps offset some of the losses. As described above, ideally the distance of the strike of the covered call compared to the stock price should be equal to approximately half of the actual loss.
    Example: The strike of the Covered Call is computed in the following way: Current Stock Price + ½ * Unrealized Loss (Original Price − Current Stock Price) = $50 + 0.5*($60-$50) = $55.
    This option is slightly out-of-the-money, allowing you to collect premium income while setting a target price for the stock to reach.
    The second component is to buy a call spread that allows you to benefit from a potential rebound while limiting further risk. The long call should be approximately at the money (0.50 delta), while the short call should have the same strike as the covered call.
    Example: The long call option that provides upside potential can be a XYZ $50 Call. The short call option that helps to reduce the cost of the long call can be a XYZ $55 Call
    - **DTE (Days to Expiration)**: Choose a timeframe that provides sufficient time for the stock to recover and for the options to work effectively. 30 days to expiration is a common choice, offering a good balance between time and premium collection.

Example: In the example the trade chooses 30 days for his strategy.

- **Execute the Trade:** You execute the trader by buying the lower strike call and selling the higher strike calls.
  Example:
    - Sell 2 x XYZ $55 Calls
    - Buy XYZ $50 Call

3.3 Adjusting the Stock Repair Strategy

Since the Stock Repair Strategy is a combination of covered call and spread, you can refer to the specific adjustments described in the previous chapters, especially if you would like to avoid assignments which will force you to sell your stock position.

As described in the previous chapters, also for the stock repair strategy it is always a viable option to completely roll out the full position (i.e. extend the overall duration of the trade) or close it early.

Regularly review the stock and option positions. Adjust as needed based on changes in stock price and market conditions. Make sure to monitor the expiration dates and adjust trades before expiration if necessary.

3.4 Estimating Capital Requirements

As described in the previous paragraph, here below the formula you can use to compute the initial capital requirement. Usually, the trader aims to setup an overall position which does not require any cost.

The capital required is primarily based on the cost of implementing the options trades.

- **Covered Call Premium**: Received premium offsets part of the cost.
- **Long Call Spread Cost**: Net cost of the spread.

Example:

- **Net Credit from Covered Call**: $95

- **Cost of Long Call Spread**: $100

- **Effective Margin Requirement**: The net cost of implementing the strategy is $100, reduced by the $95 premium received, resulting in an effective margin requirement of $5 (indicating a net cost).

3.5 CONCLUSION

The Stock Repair Strategy is a valuable tool for managing and recovering from losses on a stock position. By combining a covered call with a long call spread, traders can potentially recover from declines while managing risk effectively. This chapter provided a detailed guide to executing the strategy, including trade setup considerations (delta and DTE), adjustments, and capital estimation.

By mastering the Stock Repair Strategy, traders can enhance their ability to handle losing positions and improve their overall risk management approach. With practice and careful execution, the strategy can become a vital part of a trader's toolkit, helping to navigate challenging market conditions and recover from adverse price movements.

CHAPTER 4

THE WHEEL STRATEGY - TURNING OPPORTUNITIES INTO INCOME

In the vast world of options trading, the Wheel Strategy stands out as a popular and effective approach for generating consistent income. For many traders, the Wheel Strategy is akin to a well-oiled machine that systematically produces revenue while managing risk. This chapter delves into the purpose of the Wheel Strategy, elucidates its mechanics, and provides clear examples to illustrate its application. By the end of this chapter, you'll have a comprehensive understanding of how to implement the Wheel Strategy, optimize its performance, and adapt it to various market conditions.

The Wheel Strategy is designed to transform stock market volatility into a structured income stream. This chapter aims to:

- **Explain the Wheel Strategy**: Provide a detailed overview of the strategy, including its components and mechanics.

- **Illustrate the Strategy with Real Examples**: Show how the Wheel Strategy is applied in real-world scenarios.

- **Optimize Performance**: Offer practical tips for maximizing the effectiveness of the Wheel Strategy.

- **Adapt to Market Conditions**: Discuss how to adjust the strategy based on varying market conditions and individual trading preferences.

The Wheel Strategy can be a powerful tool for those who wish to harness the potential of options trading to generate a steady income. This chapter will provide you with the knowledge and skills necessary to deploy this strategy effectively and with confidence.

4.1 The Purpose of The Wheel Strategy

The Wheel Strategy is a popular, straightforward options trading strategy designed to generate consistent income through the systematic selling of options. It is particularly appealing to traders who are willing to own shares of a stock and are comfortable with the idea of potentially having their shares called away. The Wheel Strategy combines the sale of cash-secured puts and covered calls, allowing traders to potentially profit from both market volatility and price appreciation.

The Wheel Strategy involves a cycle of selling cash-secured put options, potentially acquiring the underlying stock, and then selling covered call options on that stock. The strategy is named "the Wheel" because it can be repeated indefinitely, cycling through these stages to generate income over time. It is considered a conservative strategy that can be attractive to investors looking for steady returns rather than aggressive growth.

- **Income Generation:** The primary purpose of the Wheel Strategy is to generate regular income through the premiums collected from selling options. Each step in the Wheel—selling puts and calls—provides an opportunity to collect premiums. These premiums can offer a steady stream of income, especially in sideways or slightly bullish markets, where the underlying stock does not experience significant price movements.

- **Acquiring Stocks at a Discount:** One of the attractive features of the Wheel Strategy is that it allows traders to potentially acquire shares of a stock at a lower price than its current market value. By selling cash-secured puts, the trader is agreeing to buy the stock at a certain price (the strike price) if the option is exercised. If the stock price falls below the strike price, the trader will be obligated to purchase the shares at that strike price, which is often lower than the market price at the time of the trade.

- **Monetizing Stock Ownership**: Once the trader owns the stock (after the put option is exercised), the next step in the Wheel Strategy is to sell covered calls. This step allows the trader to earn additional income from their stock holdings, beyond any dividends or capital appreciation. If the stock price remains stable or rises slightly, the call options may expire worthless, allowing the trader to keep the stock and the premium received.

- **Enhancing Returns in a Neutral Market:** The Wheel Strategy is particularly effective in neutral or slightly bullish markets, where significant price movements are not expected. In such environments, the steady collection of option premiums can enhance overall portfolio returns. Since the strategy involves holding or acquiring stocks that the trader is comfortable owning long-term, it aligns well with conservative investment goals.

- **Risk Management:** The Wheel Strategy also incorporates elements of risk management. By selling puts only on stocks that the trader is willing to own, the downside risk is somewhat mitigated. Additionally, selling covered calls on stocks already owned reduces the risk of holding a stock that may underperform, as the premiums from the calls provide a buffer against potential losses.

Example: Executing the Wheel Strategy

To illustrate the Wheel Strategy, let's consider a practical example involving a hypothetical stock, ABC Corp.

- **Selling the Cash-Secured Put**
    - **Stock**: ABC Corp
    - **Current Stock Price**: $52
    - **Strike Price**: $50
    - **Premium Received**: $2 per share
    - **Number of Shares**: 100

    Here, you sell a put option on ABC Corp with a strike price of $50 and receive $2 per share in premium. If ABC Corp's stock price is below $50 at expiration, you will be required to purchase the stock at $50.

- **Step 2: Acquiring the Stock (if assigned)**
    - **Stock Price at Expiration**: $48
    - **Assignment**: You buy 100 shares of ABC Corp at $50.

    Since the stock price is below the strike price, you are assigned the stock. Your effective purchase price, after accounting for the premium received, is $48 per share ($50 - $2 premium).

- **Step 3: Selling Covered Calls**
    - **Strike Price of Call**: $55
    - **Premium Received**: $1.50 per share
    - **Number of Shares**: 100

You now own the stock and sell a call option with a strike price of $55, receiving $1.50 per share in premium. If ABC Corp's stock price rises above $55, you may be obligated to sell the stock at $55.

- **Step 4: Repeating the Process**
    - **Stock Price at Expiration of Call**: $57
    - **Outcome**: The stock is called away at $55.

Since the stock price is above the call strike price, your shares are sold at $55. You repeat the process by selling another cash-secured put.

- **Overall income generated by the strategy:**
    - **Premium from the cash-secured put**: $200
    - **Premium from the covered-call**: $150
    - **Stock Appreciation**: $500
    - **Tot income**: $850

9.2 Step-by-Step Guide to Executing the Wheel Strategy

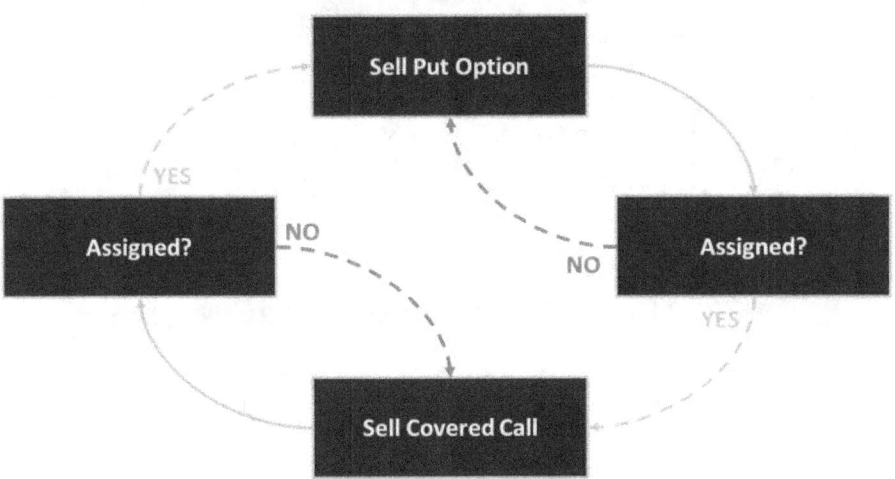

Figure 11 - Wheel Strategy Process

UNLEASH THE POWER OF ADVANCED INCOME STRATEGIES

Here's a breakdown of how the Wheel Strategy works:

1. **Sell a Cash-Secured Put**: The strategy starts by selling a put option on a stock you are willing to own. You collect a premium for this transaction, and if the stock price falls below the strike price, you may be obligated to purchase the stock.

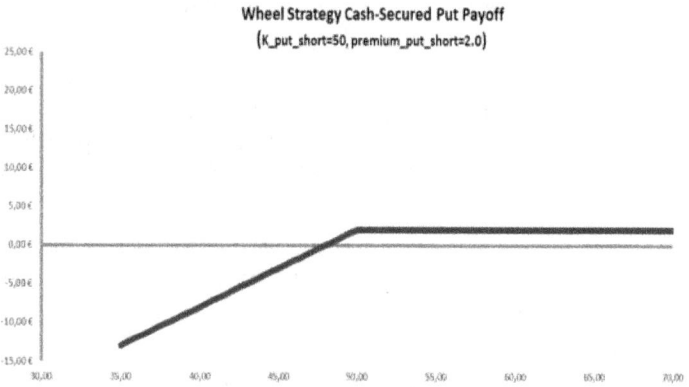

Figure 12 - Wheel Strategy Cash-Secured Put Payoff

2. **Acquire the Stock (if assigned)**: If the stock price is below the strike price at expiration, you will be assigned the stock. This means you buy the stock at the agreed-upon strike price.

3. **Sell Covered Calls**: Once you own the stock, you sell call options against it. This generates additional income through premiums. If the stock price rises above the strike price of the call option, you may be required to sell the stock.

UNLEASH THE POWER OF ADVANCED INCOME STRATEGIES

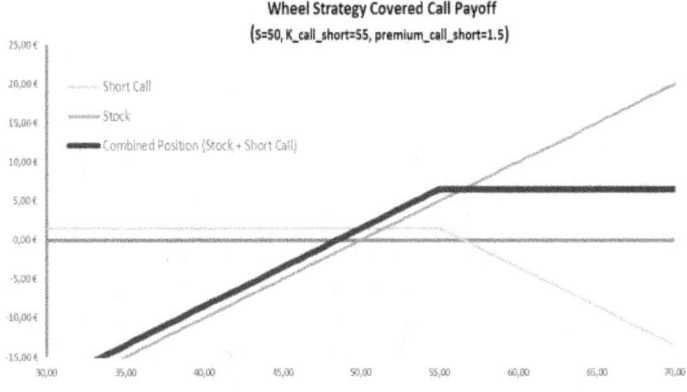

Figure 13 - Wheel Strategy Covered Call Payoff

4. **Repeat the Process**: If your stock is called away, you start the process over by selling another cash-secured put. This cyclical approach allows you to generate income continuously.

4.2.1 Choosing the Right Underlying Asset

Choosing the right stock is crucial for the success of the Wheel Strategy. Here are some factors to consider:

- **Liquidity**: Opt for stocks with high trading volumes to ensure smooth transactions and tighter bid-ask spreads.

- **Volatility**: Look for stocks with moderate to high volatility, as they generally offer higher premiums for options. Always consider that higher volatility means higher risk, as a trader you should balance the premium size and the overall risk to find the perfect balance for your position / portfolio.

- **Fundamentals**: Consider stocks with solid fundamentals and a stable outlook. This helps in reducing the risk of significant losses if the stock price declines.

Example: Suppose you're considering XYZ Corp, a well-established company with a stable earnings history and a current stock price of $60. If the stock has moderate volatility and high trading volume, it could be a good candidate for the Wheel Strategy.

4.2.2 Setting Up the Trade

The Wheel strategy requires to select the best setup for both the cash-secured and covered call options.

- **Put Strike Price**: Choose a strike price where you are comfortable buying the stock. Typically, this should be below the current stock price to ensure you receive a premium while being prepared to buy the stock at a favorable price.

- **Call Strike Price**: Set the call strike price at a level where you are willing to sell the stock. This should ideally be above the stock's current price to capture potential upside gains.

Selecting the right strike prices for both puts and calls is essential for maximizing returns and managing risk.

- **Cash-Secured Put**
    - **Delta**: For cash-secured puts, a Delta closer to -0.2 to -0.4 is often preferred. This range indicates a reasonable balance between premium collection and risk. A higher absolute Delta (e.g., -0.3) suggests a higher likelihood of assignment but also comes with a higher premium. A lower Delta (e.g., -0.2) offers less premium but a lower probability of assignment.
    Example: If XYZ Corp is trading at $50 and you decide to sell a cash-secured put with a Delta of -0.4 and a strike price of $45, you are balancing the premium received with the risk of being assigned the stock. If the stock price declines and approaches $45, the likelihood of assignment increases, and the premium you collected will compensate for this risk.
    - **DTE (Days to Expiration)**: For cash-secured puts, a typical DTE range is between 30 to 45 days. This provides enough time for the stock to potentially move in your favor while still capturing a substantial premium. A shorter DTE (e.g., 15 to 20 days) might be

used for quicker returns but could involve higher volatility and lower premiums.
Example: You sell a cash-secured put on XYZ Corp with a strike price of $45 and 35 DTE. This setup allows you to capture a significant premium while providing adequate time for the stock to potentially stay above the strike price. If the stock price stays above $45, you retain the premium without having to purchase the stock.

- **Covered Call**
  - **Delta**: For covered calls, a Delta of 0.3 to 0.5 is commonly used. This range indicates a balance between premium received and the likelihood of the call being exercised. A higher Delta (e.g., 0.5) suggests a higher chance of assignment but also a higher premium. A lower Delta (e.g., 0.3) offers a lower premium but reduces the chance of assignment. If possible, you should avoid selling call option below the stock purchase price, to avoid the risk of potential losses. If it is not possible, the trader should closely monitor the position, adjusting it to efficiently manage it (for further details, see the dedicated chapter in the first volume of the series, *The Option Trader's Income Blueprint: Master the Art of Greeks, covered Calls and Cash-Secured Puts*).
  Example: If you own XYZ Corp shares and decide to sell a covered call with a Delta of 0.4 and a strike price of $55, you are aiming for a moderate premium with a balanced probability of the call being exercised. If XYZ Corp's stock price rises to $55 or above, the call option might be exercised, and you'll have to sell your shares at the strike price.
  - **DTE (Days to Expiration)**: For covered calls, a DTE of 30 to 45 days is often ideal. This allows for a significant premium collection while providing a reasonable timeframe for the stock to potentially appreciate or stay below the strike price. A shorter DTE (e.g.,

15 to 20 days) can be used for faster returns but might result in lower premiums.

Example: You sell a covered call on XYZ Corp with a strike price of $55 and 30 DTE. If the stock price remains below $55, the call option expires worthless, and you keep the premium. If the stock price rises above $55, you may be assigned and must sell your shares, but you benefit from both the premium and the appreciation in stock price.

4.2.3 Execute the Trade

As described in the previous paragraphs, executing the Wheel Strategy involves a systematic approach, starting with the sale of a cash-secured put option on a stock you're willing to own. If the put option is exercised, you purchase the stock at the strike price, effectively acquiring it at a discount when factoring in the premium received. Once the stock is in your possession, you then sell a covered call option on the same stock, earning additional premium income.

When the strategy is initiated, the trader should monitor the position carefully:

- **Monitoring**: Continuous monitoring is crucial when implementing the Wheel Strategy. You need to keep a close eye on the price movement of the underlying stock and the expiration dates of your options. This helps you make informed decisions about when to roll a put or call option to a different strike price or expiration, based on changes in market conditions or shifts in your outlook on the stock.

- **Adjusting**: Adjusting the Wheel Strategy involves making tactical changes to your positions to manage risk or optimize returns. For instance, if the stock price declines significantly, you might roll down a put option to a lower strike price or increase your covered call's strike price if the stock shows strong upward momentum. These adjustments help maintain the strategy's effectiveness and align it with your market expectations and risk tolerance.

4.3 Adjusting the Wheel Strategy

4.3.1. Adjusting Cash-Secured Puts

You can rely on all the adjustment strategies described in the "Cash-Secured" chapter (first volume of the series, *The Option Trader's Income Blueprint: Master the Art of Greeks, covered Calls and Cash-Secured Puts*), especially:

- **Rolling the Put Option**
- **Converting the Position into a Credit Spread**
- **Exiting the Position Early**
- **Sell a Call Against the Put and Convert the Position into a Strangle / Straddle**

4.3.2 Adjusting Covered Calls

You can rely on all the adjustment strategies described in the "Covered-Call" chapter (first volume of the series, *The Option Trader's Income Blueprint: Master the Art of Greeks, covered Calls and Cash-Secured Puts*), especially:

- **Rolling the Covered Call**
- **Closing the Covered Call**
- **Converting the Position into a Collar**

4.3.4 Adjusting Based on Market Conditions

The Wheel Strategy must be adaptable to changing market conditions. Here's how to adjust your strategy:

- **Volatile Markets:** In volatile markets, stock prices can swing dramatically, impacting the performance of your positions.
  - **Increase Strike Prices:** In highly volatile markets, consider increasing the strike prices for both puts and calls to accommodate larger price swings.

- **Adjust Premiums:** Volatility often results in higher premiums. Adjust your premiums and strike prices to reflect the increased market risk.

Example: If XYZ Corp becomes more volatile, you might choose a put strike price of $52 and a call strike price of $68 to capture higher premiums and manage the increased risk.

- **Trending Markets:** In trending markets, stocks may move consistently in one direction.
  - **Trend Analysis:** Use technical analysis to identify trends and adjust your strategy accordingly.
  - **Modify Strike Prices:** In a strong uptrend, consider rolling your calls to higher strike prices to benefit from potential gains.

Example: If XYZ Corp is in a strong uptrend, you might roll your call strike price from $65 to $75 to capture additional upside potential.

- **Sideways Markets:** In sideways markets, stocks fluctuate within a narrow range.
  - **Tighten Strike Prices:** Choose strike prices closer to the current stock price to capitalize on the lack of significant price movement.
  - **Increase Frequency:** In a sideways market, you may have more frequent opportunities to implement the Wheel Strategy as stocks oscillate within a range.

Example: If XYZ Corp trades between $58 and $62, you might select put and call strike prices closer to these levels to maximize premium income.

4.3.5 Maintaining Income Generation Despite Market Drops

- **Leveraging Increased Premiums:** During market drops, the increased volatility can lead to higher premiums for both puts and calls. Utilize this to your advantage:
  - **Selling New Options**: Take advantage of higher premiums by selling new cash-

secured puts or covered calls. This helps in generating additional income, even if the stock price has declined.
- **Adjusting Strike Prices**: Use the higher premiums to adjust your strike prices and align them with the current market conditions.

Example: If the stock price of XYZ Corp has dropped, the premiums for new puts or calls will be higher. Sell new puts at a lower strike price or new calls at a higher strike price to capitalize on the increased volatility.

- **Diversifying Positions:** To mitigate the impact of a market drop on individual stocks, consider diversifying your positions:
  - **Adding New Stocks**: Incorporate additional stocks into your Wheel Strategy to spread risk.
  - **Different Expirations**: Use options with varying expiration dates to diversify the timing of potential assignments and premium collection.

Example: Alongside your position in XYZ Corp, you can start implementing the Wheel Strategy with stocks from different sectors or industries. This diversification reduces the risk of a single stock's poor performance impacting your overall strategy.

- **Strategies to handle your position after the assignment and a market drop:** When the stock price drops, the first instinct might be to sell a covered call at a lower strike price, but doing so caps your upside potential if the stock rebounds. Here below some additional strategies that can help the trader to increase the income received and mitigate the need of selling call options way below the assignment price or to mitigate the risk of the overall position:
  - **Open a Covered Call and a Ratio Spread:** If the stock drops significantly, converting your position into a ratio spread can be a viable adjustment. This involves selling multiple put options and buying fewer puts at a lower strike price:
    - **Buy Put Option:** Purchase a put option at a strike price near the current market price.
    - **Sell Two Put Options at a Lower Strike Price:** Sell two put options at a

lower strike price, creating a ratio spread that generates premium income.
- **Sell a Covered Call:** Sell a call option at a strike price above the current market price to generate premium income.

Example: Suppose XYZ drops to $40, and you buy a $40 put while selling two $35 puts. This creates a ratio spread that benefits in case of limited downside movement.

Ratio spreads generate higher return in case of limited downside. If the stock drops significantly, the risk is being assigned (one of the put is not limited by the long put).

- **Open a Covered Call and an Additional Put (Straddle):** Selling a covered call while simultaneously selling an additional put option can generate additional income while positioning you to potentially lower your average cost basis.
    - **Sell a Covered Call:** Sell a call option at a strike price above the current market price to generate premium income.
    - **Sell an Additional Cash-Secured Put:** Sell a put option at a strike price lower than the current stock price. This puts you in a position to potentially acquire more shares at a lower price, thereby averaging down your cost basis if the put is exercised.

Example: Suppose you own 100 shares of XYZ stock that you purchased at $50, but the stock has dropped to $40. You could sell a $45 strike call option, which generates premium income while still allowing some room for the stock to recover. You could sell a $35 strike put option. If the stock continues to drop and the put is exercised, you will buy another 100 shares at $35, lowering your average cost basis.

This approach generates additional premium income, reduces your average cost basis, and provides some flexibility if the stock rebounds.

The downside is that you might be assigned more shares, increasing your exposure to the stock and potential losses if the stock continues to decline.

- **Open an Additional Put Option Only:** Another adjustment strategy involves selling an additional put option without selling a covered call. This strategy is useful if you believe the stock will eventually recover, but you want to lower your cost basis without capping your upside potential. Identify a strike price where you're comfortable acquiring more shares at a lower cost. Selling this put option will generate premium income and give you the opportunity to buy more shares at a reduced price if the put is exercised.

  Example: With XYZ stock now at $40, you could sell a $35 strike put option. If assigned, you'll buy additional shares at $35, bringing down your overall cost basis.

  This approach allows you to reduce your cost basis while keeping all the upside potential if the stock recovers. It also generates immediate income from the put premium. The risk is that the stock may continue to decline, leading to further losses. Additionally, you increase your exposure to the stock by potentially doubling your position.

- **Implementing a Collar Strategy:** As described in the previous chapters, a collar strategy involves holding the stock while selling a covered call and buying a protective put. This strategy can be particularly useful if the stock drops significantly and you want to limit further downside risk while still holding the stock:

  - **Sell a Covered Call**: Sell a call option at a strike price above the current market price to generate premium income.

- **Buy a Protective Put**: Buy a put option at a strike price below the current market price to limit downside risk.

Example: If the stock is trading at $40, you could sell a $45 call and buy a $35 put. This creates a collar that limits your downside risk while allowing some upside potential if the stock recovers.

The collar strategy limits your downside risk while still allowing for some upside potential. The premium from the covered call helps offset the cost of the protective put. The collar limits your profit potential on the upside, as the stock will be called away if it rises above the call strike price.

- **Implementing a Repair Strategy:** As described in the previous chapters the repair strategy is designed to reduce the breakeven point on a stock that has declined in value, without requiring additional capital. This is done by buying a call option and selling two call options at a higher strike price (creating a ratio call spread).
  - **Buy a Call Option**: Purchase a call option at a strike price near the current market price.
  - **Sell Two Call Options at a Higher Strike Price**: Sell two call options at a higher strike price, creating a ratio spread that generates premium income.

Example: If the stock is trading at $40, you could buy a $40 call and sell two $45 calls. This lowers your breakeven point while still allowing for potential upside if the stock recovers.

The repair strategy lowers your breakeven point without requiring additional capital. It allows you to recover some losses if the stock rebounds.

The strategy limits your profit potential, as the stock may be called away if it rises above the higher strike price. There is also the risk of a significant rally causing the short calls to be exercised.

4.3.6 Case Studies

Case Study: Market Drop Scenario (KO)

Background: Jane, an experienced options trader, implemented the Wheel Strategy on KO. Initially, she sold a cash-secured put with a strike price of $50. The stock price then dropped to $45, and Jane was assigned the stock.

Adjustment:

- **Rolling Down**: Jane rolled her original put to a lower strike price of $40, extending the expiration date to capture higher premiums.
- **Covered Call**: After acquiring the stock, Jane sold a covered call with a strike price of $50, adjusting the strike price to reflect the new market conditions.

Outcome:

- The increased premiums from the rolled put provided additional income.
- The covered call was less likely to be exercised but generated premium income that offset some of the stock's decline.

Case Study: Protecting Against Further Declines (EBAY)

Background: Mark was assigned shares of EBAY at $60 after selling a cash-secured put. The stock price then fell to $55.

Adjustment:

- **Protective Put:** Mark purchased a protective put with a strike price of $50 to hedge against further declines.
- **Rolling Covered Call:** Mark rolled his covered call down to a strike price of $55 to capture additional premium.

Outcome:

UNLEASH THE POWER OF ADVANCED INCOME STRATEGIES

- The protective put limited Mark's losses as the stock continued to decline.
- The rolled call position provided extra premium income, helping to offset the stock's drop.

4.4 ESTIMATING CAPITAL REQUIREMENTS

As described at the beginning of the chapter, the trader should be ready to buy 100 share of the underlying asset at the pre-defined strike price (cash-secured put) in case of assignment.

In the step-by-step example previously reported, the overall capital requirement was approximately 100 x $50 = $5000.

4.5 CASE STUDY – WHEEL STRATEGY ON MSFT

Case Study: Wheel Strategy on MSFT

Step 1: Selecting the Stock

- **Stock:** Microsoft Corporation (MSFT)
- **Current Price (as of the latest data):** $340 per share

Step 2: Selling Cash-Secured Puts

Option Details

- **Strike Price:** $330 (slightly out-of-the-money)
- **Premium Received:** $5.50 per share
- **Expiration:** 30 days

Capital Requirement:

- For 1 contract (100 shares), you need $33,000 (cash to secure the put)

Potential Outcome 1: Put Expires Worthless

- **Income Earned:** $550 (premium received)
- **Annualized Return:** (assuming this can be repeated monthly) = 550/3300 * 12 = **20%**

Potential Outcome 2: Assigned the Stock

- **Stock Purchase Price:** $330 per share
- **Effective Cost Basis:** $324.50 (Strike Price - Premium Received)

Step 3: Selling Covered Calls (if stock assigned in the previous step)

Covered Call Details:

- **Strike Price:** $340
- **Premium Received:** $5.50 per share
- **Expiration:** 30 days

Capital Requirement:

- Already holding 100 shares of MSFT at $330

Potential Outcome 1: Call Expires Worthless

- **Income Earned:** $550 (call premium)
- **Annualized Return:** Annualized Return= 550/32450 * 12= **20.3%**

Potential Outcome 2: Stock Called Away

- **Call Premium:** $550
- **Capital Gain:** $10 per share (Strike Price - Effective Cost Basis)
- **Total Gain:** $1,550 ($550 call premium + $1,000 capital gain)
- **Annualized Return:** Annualized Return= 1550/32450* 12 = **57.3%**

4.6 Conclusion

The Wheel Strategy offers a systematic approach to options trading that can generate consistent income while managing risk. By understanding the mechanics of selling cash-secured puts and covered calls, optimizing your trade setups, and adapting to market conditions, you can effectively harness the power of this strategy. With practice and experience, the Wheel Strategy can become a valuable tool in your options trading toolkit, providing a structured pathway to achieving financial goals.

CHAPTER 5

LEAPS OPTIONS – ENHANCING YOUR STRATEGY WITH LONG-TERM LEVERAGE

Imagine having the ability to control a significant amount of stock with a fraction of the capital typically required for outright ownership. This is the allure of LEAPS (Long-Term Equity Anticipation Securities), a powerful tool that offers a strategic advantage for investors seeking to maximize returns with limited risk exposure. In this chapter, we delve into the world of LEAPS, exploring how these long-term options can enhance your trading strategy, particularly when compared to directly owning the underlying stock.

5.1 THE PURPOSE OF LEAPS

LEAPS are options contracts with expiration dates that are significantly longer than the typical short-term options, often extending up to two years or more. While standard options typically have expiration dates ranging from a few weeks to a few months, LEAPS provide an extended timeframe, allowing traders to take a longer-term view on the underlying asset.

- **Expiration Dates**: LEAPS generally have expiration dates ranging from 9 months to 2 years in the future.

- **Strike Prices**: Like standard options, LEAPS come with various strike prices that determine the level at which the option can be exercised or assigned.

- **Premiums**: Due to their longer duration, LEAPS typically have higher premiums compared to short-term options. However, they also offer greater potential for significant price movements.

Example: Suppose you are bullish on XYZ Corp, which is currently trading at $100. Instead of buying 100 shares at $10,000, you could purchase a LEAPS call option with a strike price of $110 and an expiration date two years out. The premium for this LEAPS option might be $10 per share, costing you $1,000 for the option. This allows you to control the equivalent of 100 shares for a fraction of the cost.

5.2 WHY USE LEAPS INSTEAD OF THE UNDERLYING STOCK?

Using LEAPS instead of the underlying stock can give the traders several benefits, here below the main ones:

- **Capital Efficiency:** LEAPS offer a more capital-efficient way to gain exposure to the underlying stock. By using LEAPS, you can control a significant amount of stock for a fraction of the price, preserving your capital for other investments or opportunities.
  Example: Owning 100 shares of XYZ Corp at $100 per share costs $10,000. In contrast, buying a LEAPS call option might cost $1,000 for the same exposure, allowing you to allocate the remaining $9,000 elsewhere.
  Example: You are considering investing in ABC Inc., which is currently trading at $50 per share. Instead of purchasing 200 shares for $10,000, you could buy LEAPS calls with a strike price of $55, expiring in 18 months. If the premium for these LEAPS calls is $6 per share, the total cost would be $1,200, giving you control over the equivalent of 200 shares for a significantly lower investment.

- **Leveraged Exposure:** LEAPS provide leverage, which can amplify returns if the underlying stock moves in your favor. This leverage means that a relatively small movement in the stock price can result in a significant percentage gain in the LEAPS option.
  Example: If XYZ Corp's stock price increases from $100 to $120, the LEAPS call option with a $110 strike price could increase in

value substantially, even if the price movement is relatively small compared to the underlying stock.

Example: Assume you buy LEAPS calls on XYZ Corp with a $110 strike price for $5 per share. If the stock rises to $120, the intrinsic value of the LEAPS call becomes $10 per share, resulting in a profit of $5 per share, or a 100% return on your investment.

- **Long-Term View:** LEAPS are ideal for investors with a long-term bullish outlook on the underlying stock. They allow you to capitalize on long-term trends without having to commit the capital required to buy and hold the stock outright.

  Example: If you believe in the long-term growth prospects of ABC Corp, purchasing DEF LEAPS calls allows you to benefit from potential future price increases over an extended period, without worrying about short-term volatility.

  Example: You anticipate that ABC Corp will grow substantially over the next two years due to an innovative product launch. Instead of buying shares and holding them, you purchase LEAPS calls with a strike price of $60, expiring in 24 months. As the company's value grows, the LEAPS calls can appreciate significantly, offering substantial returns.

5.3 How to Use LEAPS in Your Trading Strategy

The trader can decide to use the LEAPS in different strategies, here below some of the most used:

- **Incorporating LEAPS into the Wheel Strategy:** The Wheel Strategy involves selling cash-secured puts to potentially acquire stock and then selling covered calls to generate income. LEAPS can be used to enhance this strategy by providing long-term exposure to the stock while reducing the capital required.

  Sell cash-secured puts on the underlying stock to potentially acquire shares. Once you own the shares, you can sell covered calls, or alternatively, use LEAPS calls to benefit from long-term appreciation without having to hold the stock. The LEAPS call should be deep in the money, in order to ensure that its delta is comparable to the stock one (i.e. LEAPS call delta should be higher than 80/90).

  Example: You sell cash-secured puts on XYZ Corp with a strike price of $45. If assigned, you acquire the stock and then sell

UNLEASH THE POWER OF ADVANCED INCOME STRATEGIES

covered calls. Instead of holding the stock, you could use LEAPS calls to benefit from long-term appreciation, while selling shorter-term calls to generate additional income.

- **Using LEAPS for Long-Term Bullish Positions:** If you have a strong long-term bullish outlook on a stock, LEAPS can provide an effective way to capitalize on that belief with reduced risk and lower capital requirements.
    - **Setup – Alternative 1**: Purchase LEAPS calls with a strike price deep in the money (i.e. 80/90). This will make the option behave similarly to the underlying asset, even if the cost to buy it is just a fraction.
    - **Setup – Alternative 2**: Purchase LEAPS calls with a strike slightly out of the money (i.e. 40/30). The cost of the option will be lower, but to make the strategy earn some profits the underlying price should increase a lot more.

The trader should find the right balance between cost and risk, in order to find the best approach that fits with the expectations about the underlying asset

Example: You believe that XYZ Inc. will see substantial growth over the next two years. Instead of buying shares, you buy a deep in the money LEAPS call with a two-year expiration. As the stock rises, the value of the LEAPS calls increases, providing you with leveraged exposure to the stock's long-term appreciation.

5.4 MANAGING LEAPS POSITIONS

Proper management of LEAPS positions involves monitoring the stock's performance, adjusting strike prices, and considering the impact of time decay.

- **Monitoring**: Track the performance of the underlying stock and the LEAPS option to assess the value and adjust your strategy as needed.

- **Adjustments**: If the stock price approaches the strike price, consider rolling up to higher strike prices or extending the expiration to capture additional potential gains. You can always roll the position if you want to keep the theta decay under control (i.e. if you buy a long LEAPs call option, the theta decay act against you, so you can roll the position out in order to keep it under control – as described in the previous chapters (first volume of the series, *The Option Trader's Income Blueprint: Master the Art of Greeks, covered Calls and Cash-Secured Puts*), the effect of the theta is higher when the position gets close to the expiration)

Example: If you hold LEAPS calls on JKL Corp with a $50 strike price, and the stock price rises to $60, you may consider rolling up to a $65 strike price to lock in profits while maintaining exposure to further price increases.

5.5 Practical Considerations and Examples

Here below some practical consideration a trader can consider when using LEAPS:

- **Choosing the Right LEAPS:** When selecting LEAPS options, consider the following factors:
    - **Strike Price**: Choose a strike price that aligns with your long-term outlook and risk tolerance. In-the-money LEAPS provide higher intrinsic value but cost more, while out-of-the-money LEAPS are cheaper but riskier.
    - **Expiration Date**: Select an expiration date that matches your investment horizon and expected time frame for price movements.

  Example: You are interested in investing in RST Corp, which is currently trading at $80. You anticipate significant growth over the next 18 months. You could choose LEAPS calls with a strike price of $85 and an expiration date 18 months out. This provides a balance between cost and potential for profit.

- **Risk Management:** While LEAPS offer significant advantages, they also come with risks. Effective risk management involves:
    - **Diversification**: Avoid concentrating too much capital in a single LEAPS position. Diversify across different stocks and sectors to spread risk.
    - **Monitoring**: Regularly review your LEAPS positions and the underlying stock's performance. Be prepared to adjust or exit positions based on market conditions and changes in your outlook.

Example: You hold LEAPS calls on two different stocks, PQR Inc. and STU Corp. If PQR Inc. experiences a sharp decline, you can focus on managing the LEAPS position in STU Corp, which may still be performing well. Diversification helps mitigate losses from individual stock declines.

5.6 CONCLUSION

LEAPS provide a unique opportunity to participate in long-term market movements with a fraction of the capital required for stock ownership. They offer the potential for significant returns through leverage, while also allowing for strategic adjustments to manage risk.

CHAPTER 6

ALTERNATIVE WHEEL STRATEGY WITH CREDIT SPREADS

In the realm of options trading, the Wheel Strategy is a popular method that systematically generates income by cycling through different stages of selling puts and calls. However, traders who seek to modify and enhance this strategy may consider incorporating credit spreads. This chapter will delve into the alternative Wheel Strategy using credit spreads, offering a comprehensive guide to executing the trade, setting it up with delta and DTE considerations, adjusting, and estimating the required capital.

6.1 THE PURPOSE OF THE WHEEL STRATEGY WITH CREDIT SPREADS

The traditional Wheel Strategy involves three main stages:

1. **Selling Cash-Secured Puts**: To acquire stock at a lower price.

2. **Selling Covered Calls**: To earn income if the stock price rises.

3. **Repeating the Cycle**: Upon assignment, repeat the process by selling cash-secured puts on the new stock position.

The Alternative Wheel Strategy with credit spreads enhances this approach by using vertical credit spreads instead of selling outright puts and calls. This adjustment helps manage risk by limiting potential losses and offers a more structured way to profit from both stock movements and option premiums.

Credit Spreads involve buying and selling options with the same expiration date but different strike prices. They are classified into two main types:

- **Bull Put Spread**: Selling a higher strike put and buying a lower strike put to limit potential losses.

- **Bear Call Spread**: Selling a lower strike call and buying a higher strike call to cap potential losses on the upside.

Incorporating credit spreads into the Wheel Strategy allows traders to benefit from premium collection while managing risk more effectively.

Let's walk through a detailed example using the Alternative Wheel Strategy with credit spreads, focusing on a hypothetical stock, ABC Inc.

- **Selling a Put Credit Spread:**
    - **Stock**: ABC Corp
    - **Current Stock Price**: $52
    - **Sell a Put Credit Spread ($50 / $47)**
    - **Premium Received from the Credit Spread**: $0.8 per share

You sell a put credit spread on ABC Corp with a strike price of $50/$47 and receive $0.8 per share in premium.

If ABC Corp's stock price is below $50 at expiration, the trader collects the premium received at the beginning of the trade and start the process again.

If ABC Corp's stock price is below $50 at expiration, you will have the following options:

- Stock price between the put spread ($50/$47): you can decide to close the spread before assignment with a loss or wait till the expiration and receive the underlying asset. If you choose to close the spread, you'll start again with Step 1, otherwise you will proceed with the next steps of the Wheel strategy. Be aware that in the second case (assignment), the long call reduced the overall profitability, so the overall cost basis of the position is higher if compared to the same situation with the Standard Wheel Strategy. This should be considered when you'll choose the strike of the call options in the next phase of the Wheel Strategy.
- Stock price below the long put ($47): you can decide to let the position expire (no

assignment) or close the long side of the spread and get the assignment. If you choose the first option, you'll start again with Step 1, otherwise you will proceed with the next step of the Wheel Strategy. Be aware that in the second case (assignment), the long call mitigated the loss, so the overall cost basis of the position is lower if compared to the same situation with the Standard Wheel Strategy. This will help you lower the strike of the call options in the next phase of the Wheel Strategy.

- **Acquiring the Stock (if assigned):**
    - **Stock Price at Expiration**: $48
    - **Assignment**: You buy 100 shares of ABC Corp at $50.

Since the stock price is below the strike price, you are assigned the stock. Your effective purchase price, after accounting for the premium received, is $49.2 per share ($50 - $0.8 premium).

- **Selling a Call Credit Spread:**
    - **Current Stock Price**: $48
    - **Sell a Call Credit Spread ($50 / $53)**
    - **Premium Received from the Credit Spread**: $0.8 per share

You now own the stock and sell a call credit spread with a strike price of $50/$53, receiving $0.8 per share in premium.

If possible, please ensure that the short strike price is at least equal to the cost basis of the overall position ($49.2). If it is not possible, manage the position with the same strategies described in the previous chapter about the Standard Wheel Strategy.
If ABC Corp's stock price is above $50 at expiration, you will have the following options:
- Stock price between the call spread ($50/$53): you can wait till the expiration and you will be forced to sell the underlying asset.
- Stock price above the long call ($53): you can close the entire position (stock + credit spread). In this situation the overall profit is

higher compared to the Standard Wheel Strategy cause above the long strike the profits coming from the appreciation of the underlying asset are no longer counterbalanced by effect of the credit spread.

- **Repeating the Process:**
  - **Stock Price at Expiration of Call**: $57
  - **Outcome**: You close the entire position.

You can now repeat the process by selling another put credit spread.

- **Overall income generated by the strategy:**
  - **Premium from the put credit spread**: $80
  - **Premium from the call credit spread**: $80
  - **Stock Appreciation**: $400 ($57-$53 = $4.00, since in the $50/$53 range the stock profits are counterbalanced by the loss coming from the short call spread)
  - **Tot income:** $560

6.2 STEP-BY-STEP GUIDE TO EXECUTING THE ALTERNATIVE WHEEL STRATEGY WITH CREDIT SPREADS

Here's a breakdown of how to integrate spreads into the Wheel Strategy:

- **Selling a Put Credit Spread**: Instead of selling a single cash-secured put, you can sell a put credit spread. This involves selling a put option at a higher strike price while simultaneously buying a put option at a lower strike price. The goal is to collect a premium while limiting potential losses.

  The put credit spread reduces the capital requirement compared to a cash-secured put, as the maximum loss is capped by the long put. This makes it a more capital-efficient way to generate income while managing downside risk.

UNLEASH THE POWER OF ADVANCED INCOME STRATEGIES

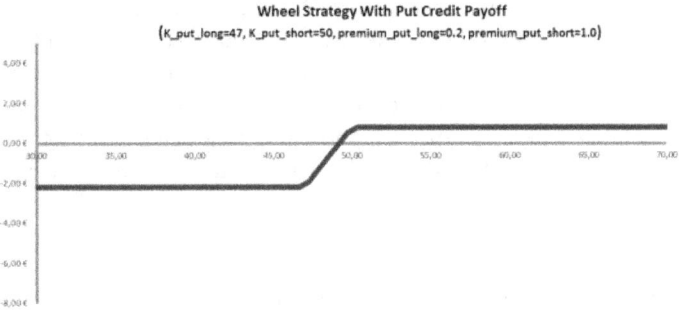

Figure 14 - Wheel Strategy With Put Credit Spread Payoff

- **Transitioning to Covered Call Spread (Bear Call Spread):** If the put credit spread expires in-the-money and you are assigned the stock, you now own the shares. Instead of selling a naked covered call, you can implement a bear call spread, which involves selling a call at a higher strike price and buying a call at an even higher strike price.

  The bear call spread provides income through the sale of the call while limiting the potential loss if the stock price rises sharply. This creates a defined risk scenario, making the strategy more conservative.

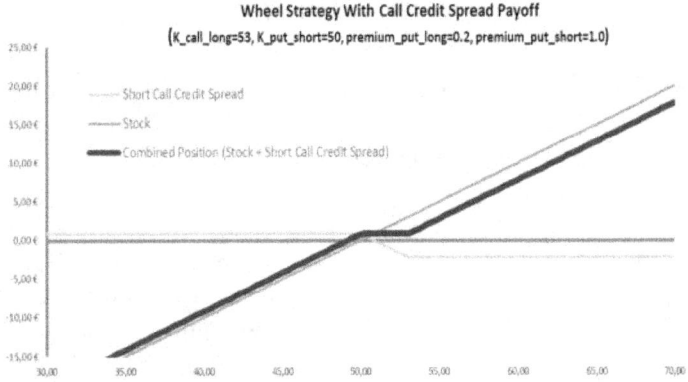

Figure 15 - Wheel Strategy With Call Credit Spread Payoff

- **Rolling and Adjusting the Spreads:** As with the traditional Wheel Strategy, rolling and adjusting are essential. You may choose to

roll your spreads to later expiration dates or different strike prices if the market moves against you or to capture more premium.
Rolling spreads allow for better risk management and income optimization. For instance, if your put spread is close to being in-the-money, you could roll it to a lower strike price and a further expiration to stay in the trade with adjusted risk.

6.2.1 Choosing the Right Underlying Asset

With the Alternative Wheel Strategy with Credit Spreads there is no relevant difference compared to the logics already described for the Wheel Strategy.

The same key variables should be considered also for the new version of the Wheel Strategy:

- **Liquidity**
- **Volatility**
- **Fundamentals**

Please refer to the Wheel Strategy chapter for further insights.

6.2.2 Setting the Trade

Here below the main setups for the ratio spreads:

- **Put Spread:**
    - **Delta:** For the Bull Spread, generally, the delta of the short put minus the delta of the long put. Usually, a trader can choose approximately -0.4/-0.3 delta for the short put and -0.2/-0.15 for the long one.
    - **DTE (Days to Expiration):** Choosing an appropriate expiration date is crucial. For this example, a 30-day expiration aligns with the typical timeframe for credit spreads. 30 DTE balances premium collection and time for stock price movement.

- **Call Spread:**
  - **Delta:** For the Bear Spread, generally, the delta of the short call minus the delta of the long call. Usually, a trader can choose approximately 0.4/0.3 delta for the short call and 0.2/0.15 for the long one.
  - **DTE (Days to Expiration):** Choosing an appropriate expiration date is crucial. For this example, a 30-day expiration aligns with the typical timeframe for credit spreads. 30 DTE balances premium collection and time for stock price movement.

6.2.3 Execute the Trade

To execute the Alternative Wheel Strategy with Credit Spreads, the trader follows the same systematic approach described in the Wheel Strategy chapter, but using credit spreads (put credit spread and call credit spread) instead of cash-secured puts and covered calls.

When the trade is executed, the trader should monitor it carefully to ensure that the position can be adjusted and managed in the best way possible.

- **Monitoring**: When using credit spreads within the Wheel Strategy, it's essential to keep a close watch on both the underlying stock's price and the spread's value. Regularly check how close the stock price is to the short strike of your spread, as approaching this level may increase the risk of assignment or reduce the profitability of the trade. Monitoring implied volatility is also crucial, as changes can significantly impact the spread's value and the likelihood of hitting your strike prices.

- **Adjusting**: Adjustments in the Wheel Strategy with credit spreads often involve rolling the spread to a different strike price or expiration to manage risk or capture additional premium. If the stock price moves against your position, you might roll the spread to a lower strike (for puts) or higher strike (for calls) to avoid assignment and maintain a favorable risk-reward ratio. You could also adjust by closing the current spread and opening a new one at a more advantageous strike price to better align with the stock's new trading range or volatility environment.

6.3 Adjustments and Management

The Wheel Strategy with Credit Spreads relies on the Standard Wheel Strategy method and enhance it with the usage of Credit Spreads.

Therefore, the adjustment described in the specific chapters (Wheel Strategy / Credit Spreads) can be applied to the Wheel Strategy with Credit Spreads.

6.4 Estimating Capital Requirements

The initial capital required for the strategy is reduced compared to the one needed to execute the Standard Wheel Strategy because of the usage of the credit spreads (which require lower capital allocation).

Anyway, since it is possible (and expected) to be assigned during the execution of the strategy, the trader should be able to afford to buy 100 shares of the underlying asset (exactly as it happens with the Standard Wheel Strategy).

In the example reported above, the overall capital required is approximately 100 x $50 = $5000.

6.5 Conclusion

The Alternative Wheel Strategy with credit spreads provides a sophisticated way to generate income while managing risk. By replacing the traditional cash-secured puts and covered calls with credit spreads, traders can benefit from premium collection while limiting potential losses.

This chapter has offered a step-by-step guide to executing the trade, including trade setup considerations (delta and DTE), adjustment strategies, and estimating the capital requirements. Mastering this strategy enables traders to enhance their income-generating potential and manage risk more effectively. By understanding and applying these concepts, you can refine your trading approach and achieve more consistent and controlled outcomes in your options trading endeavors.

CHAPTER 7

ALTERNATIVE WHEEL STRATEGY WITH RATIO SPREADS

The Wheel Strategy is a classic options trading strategy that involves selling puts to acquire stock and then selling covered calls on the acquired stock. To enhance this technique, we can integrate Ratio Spreads into the Wheel Strategy, offering an advanced and sophisticated approach that improves risk management, capital efficiency, and potential returns.

This chapter provides a comprehensive, step-by-step guide to implementing the Alternative Wheel Strategy using Put Ratio Spreads and Call Ratio Spreads. We will explore the mechanics of these spreads, discuss how they can be used within the Wheel framework, and provide clear examples to illustrate the strategy's potential.

7.1 THE PURPOSE OF THE WHEEL STRATEGY WITH RATIO SPREADS

The traditional Wheel Strategy involves three main stages:

1. **Selling Cash-Secured Puts**: To acquire stock at a lower price.

2. **Selling Covered Calls**: To earn income if the stock price rises.

3. **Repeating the Cycle**: Upon assignment, repeat the process by selling cash-secured puts on the new stock position.

The Wheel Strategy with ratio spreads offers a unique risk-return profile. While it enhances income through higher premiums, it also introduces additional complexity and risk. The potential for loss is higher if the stock price moves significantly beyond the strike prices of the ratio spread. However, the structured nature of the spreads helps to cap losses and optimize the risk-reward balance.

This strategy is particularly effective in markets with low to moderate volatility, where the stock price is expected to remain within a specific range. Traders must carefully assess market conditions and the underlying stock's volatility before implementing the strategy.

Ratio Spreads involve buying and selling options with the same expiration date but different strike prices. They are classified into two main types:

- **Put Ratio Spread**: Buying a higher strike put and selling two lower strike puts.

- **Call Ratio Spread**: Buying a lower strike call and selling two higher strike calls.

Incorporating credit spreads into the Wheel Strategy allows traders to benefit from premium collection, while managing risk effectively (the structure of the ratio spread helps to reduce potential losses, while allowing for significant profit potential if the stock price moves within a specific range).

Let's walk through a detailed example using the Alternative Wheel Strategy with credit spreads, focusing on a hypothetical stock, ABC Inc.

- **Selling a Put Ratio Spread:**
    - **Stock**: ABC Corp
    - **Current Stock Price**: $52
    - **Put Ratio Spread:** Buy 1 50 put ($1.00), Sell 2 47 puts ($0.70)
    - **Premium Received**: $0.40 per share (0.70*2-1.00 = $0.40)

In this scenario, the trader initiates the Wheel Strategy by selling a put ratio spread on ABC Corp.

If ABC Corp's stock price is below $50 at expiration, the trader collects the premium received (generally lower if compared to the standard Wheel strategy or the Credit Spread version) at the beginning of the trade and start the process again.

If ABC Corp's stock price is below $50 at expiration, you will have the following options:

- Stock price between the put spread ($50/$47): the 50 put is in the money and the 47 puts are out of the money. The

position profits from the long spread (1 long 50 put / 1 short 47 put) and the process can be started over again. The remaining short 47 put will expire worthless.
- Stock price below the short put ($47): in this situation, the long spread (1 long 50 put / 1 short 47 put) will achieve maximum profit, while the remaining short 47 put will be in the money.

The trader can decide to keep the position open and get the stock assigned at expiration, or close early the position (exactly as it happens with a standard Wheel Strategy). Anyway, the profit coming from the long spread will reduce the overall loss.

- **Acquiring the Stock (if assigned):**
    - **Stock Price at Expiration**: $45
    - **Assignment**: You buy 100 shares of ABC Corp at $47.

Since the stock price is below the strike price, you are assigned the stock. Your effective purchase price, after accounting for the premium received, is $43.6 (short put strike price - initial premium - profit from long spread (1 long 50 put / 1 short 47 put) = $47.0 - $0.40 - $3.0 = $43.6) per share. Also in this scenario, the PL of the position is still positive and the trader gain some profits even if the stock is assigned. Of course, in case of further price reduction of the underlying asset, the trader could incur in losses.

- **Selling a Call Ratio Spread:**
    - **Current Stock Price**: $45
    - **Sell a Call Ratio Spread:** Buy 1 47 call ($1.00), Sell 2 50 calls ($0.70)
    - **Premium Received**: $0.40 per share (0.70*2-1.00 = $0.40)

You now own the stock and sell a call ratio spread with a strike price of $47/$50, receiving $0.4 per share in premium.

If possible, please ensure that the short strike price is at least equal to the cost basis of the overall position ($43.6). If it is not possible, manage the position with the same strategies described in the previous chapter about the Standard Wheel Strategy.

If ABC Corp's stock price is above $47 at expiration, you will have the following options:
- Stock price between the call spread ($47/$50): the 47 call is in the money and the 50 puts are out of the money. The position profits from the long spread (1 long 47 call / 1 short 50 call) and the stock appreciation. The trader should close the ratio position (or at least the long spread) before expiration, otherwise he will be assigned at expiration, thus increasing the overall stock position. Afterwards, the trader can proceed again by selling another call ratio spread. In this scenario, the trader will benefit also from the stock appreciation.
- Stock price above the short call ($50): the position will gain maximum profit from the long spread (1 long 47 call / 1 short 50 call). The trader will benefit from the stock appreciation until the price goes beyond the short call strike. Further stock gains will be capped by the remaining short 50 call. The stock will be called away at expiration.

- **Repeating the Process:**
    - **Stock Price at Expiration of Call**: $53
    - **Outcome**: You close the entire position.

You can now repeat the process by selling another put credit spread.

- **Overall income generated by the strategy:**
    - **Income from the put ratio spread**: $340
    - **income from the call ratio spread**: $340
    - **Stock Appreciation**: $300 ($50-$47=$3, beyond $50 the profits coming from the stock appreciation are capped by the short $50 call)
    - **Tot income: $980**

7.2 STEP-BY-STEP GUIDE TO EXECUTING THE ALTERNATIVE WHEEL STRATEGY WITH CREDIT SPREADS

Integrating Ratio Spreads into the Wheel Strategy provides a way to generate income while managing risk effectively and potentially improving the possibility to gain larger profit in specific market conditions (slight movement of the stock). The strategy begins with a Put Ratio Spread instead of a simple cash-secured put and transitions to a Call Ratio Spread instead of a covered call.

- **Selling a Put Ratio Spread**: Instead of selling a single cash-secured put, you can sell a put ratio spread. This involves buying a put option at a higher strike price while simultaneously selling two put options at a lower strike price. The goal is to generate income through the net premium received, while increasing the opportunity of profit in case of price reduction given the payoff of the ratio spread.

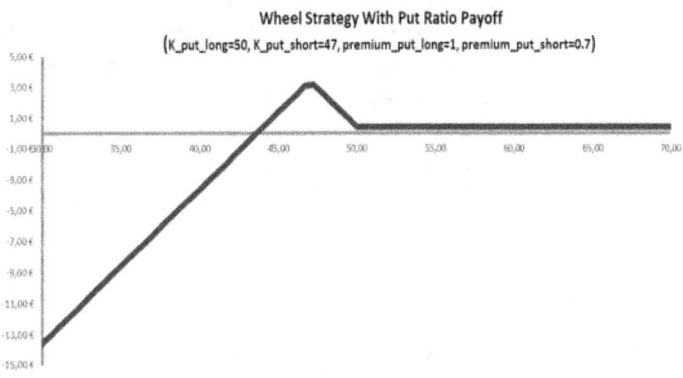

Figure 16 - Wheel Strategy With Put Ratio Payoff

- **Transitioning to Covered Call Ratio Spread**: If the stock is assigned in the previous step, you now own the shares. Instead of selling a naked covered call, you can implement a call ratio spread, which involves buying a call at a higher strike price and selling two calls at an even higher strike price.
The position provides income through the sale of the calls and can increase the profits in case of slight upside movements of the underlying asset.

UNLEASH THE POWER OF ADVANCED INCOME STRATEGIES

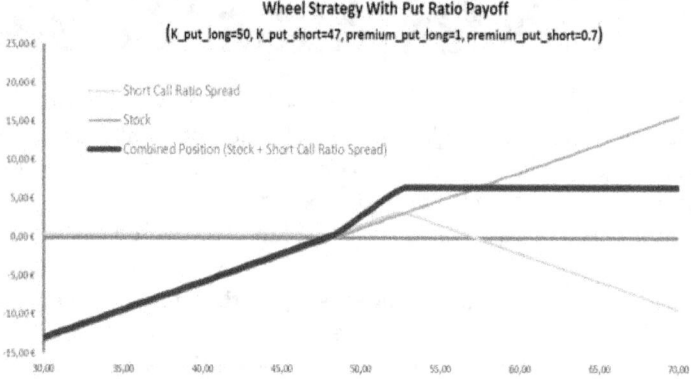

Figure 17 - Wheel Strategy With Call Ratio Payoff

- **Rolling and Adjusting the Spreads:** As with the traditional Wheel Strategy, rolling and adjusting are essential. You may choose to roll your ratio spreads to later expiration dates or different strike prices if the market moves against you or to capture more premium.
Rolling ratio spreads allow for better risk management and income optimization.

7.2.1 Choosing the Right Underlying Asset

With the Alternative Wheel Strategy with Ratio Spreads there is no relevant difference compared to the logics already described for the Wheel Strategy / Wheel Strategy with Credit Spreads.

The same key variables should be considered also for the new version of the Wheel Strategy:

- Liquidity
- Volatility
- Fundamentals

Please refer to the Wheel Strategy chapter for further insights.

7.2.2 Setting the Trade

Here below the main setups for the ratio spreads:

- **Put Ratio Spread:**
    - **Delta:** Usually, a trader can choose approximately -0.5/-0.4 delta for the long put and -0.2/-0.3 for the short ones.
    - **DTE (Days to Expiration):** Choosing an appropriate expiration date is crucial. For this example, a 30-day / 45-days expiration aligns with the typical timeframe for ratio spreads. 30/45 DTE balances premium collection and time for stock price movement.

- **Call Ratio Spread:**
    - **Delta:** Usually, a trader can choose approximately 0.5/0.4 delta for the long call and 0.3/0.2 for the short ones.
    - **DTE (Days to Expiration):** Choosing an appropriate expiration date is crucial. For this example, a 30-day / 45-days expiration aligns with the typical timeframe for ratio spreads. 45 DTE balances premium collection and time for stock price movement.

7.2.3 Execute the Trade

To execute the Alternative Wheel Strategy with Ratio Spreads, the trader follows the same systematic approach described in the Wheel Strategy chapter, but using ratio spreads instead of cash-secured puts and covered calls.

When the trade is executed, the trader should monitor it carefully to ensure that the position can be adjusted and managed in the best way possible.

- **Monitoring:** When using ratio spreads within the Wheel Strategy, it's essential to keep a close watch on both the underlying stock's price and the ratio spread's value. Regularly check how close the stock price is to the short strike of your spread, as approaching this level may increase the risk of assignment or reduce the profitability of the trade. Monitoring implied volatility is also crucial, as changes can significantly impact the spread's value and the likelihood of hitting your strike prices.

- **Adjusting**: Adjustments in the Wheel Strategy with ratio spreads often involve rolling the spread to a different strike price or expiration to manage risk or capture additional premium. If the stock price moves against your position, you might roll the spread to a lower strike (for puts) or higher strike (for calls) to avoid assignment and maintain a favorable risk-reward ratio. You could also adjust by closing the current spread and opening a new one at a more advantageous strike price to better align with the stock's new trading range or volatility environment. The ratio spreads can help the trader reduce the cost basis in case of adjustment thanks to the embedded long spread.

7.3 Adjustments and Management

The Wheel Strategy with Ratio Spreads relies on the Standard Wheel Strategy method and enhance it with the usage of Ratio Spreads.
Therefore, the adjustment described in the specific chapters (Wheel Strategy / Ratio Spreads) can be applied to the Wheel Strategy with Ratio Spreads.

7.4 Estimating Capital Requirements

The initial capital required for the strategy is slightly reduced compared to the one needed to execute the Standard Wheel Strategy because of the usage of the ratio spreads.

Anyway, since it is possible (and expected) to be assigned during the execution of the strategy, the trader should be able to afford to buy 100 shares of the underlying asset (exactly as it happens with the Standard Wheel Strategy).

In the example reported above, the overall capital required is approximately 100 x $47 = $4700.

7.5 Conclusion

The Alternative Wheel Strategy with ratio spreads provides a sophisticated way to generate income while managing risk. By replacing the traditional cash-secured puts and covered calls with ratio spreads, traders can benefit from premium collection while increasing the potential profits in specific market scenarios.

This chapter has provided a detailed, step-by-step guide to executing the Wheel Strategy with ratio spreads, covering critical elements such as trade setup considerations (including optimal delta and days to expiration), adjustment techniques, and capital requirement estimation. Mastery of these concepts equips traders with the tools to significantly improve their income-generating capabilities. By applying these advanced strategies, you can refine your trading approach, enhance consistency, and achieve more profitable outcomes in your options trading ventures.

CHAPTER 8

WHEEL STRATEGIES: A COMPREHENSIVE COMPARISON

This comparative table outlines the differences between the standard Wheel Strategy, the Wheel Strategy with Credit Spreads, and the Wheel Strategy with Ratio Spreads. This table considers various aspects such as strategy goal and mindset, entry and exit psychology, pros, and cons.

8.1 WHEEL STRATEGIES COMPARISON

This table provides a clear overview of the various Wheel Strategy alternatives:

- **Strategy Goal and Mindset:** Each strategy has a different approach to balancing risk and reward, with the standard Wheel focusing on simplicity and consistent premiums, while the variations aim to enhance returns or reduce capital requirements with more sophisticated structures.

- **Expected Market Environment:** Each strategy works best in different market conditions, with the standard Wheel being suited for stable or slightly bullish markets, Credit Spreads for moderate volatility, and Ratio Spreads for environments with higher volatility.

- **Expected Exit:** The standard Wheel is focused on simple, favorable outcomes, while the spread-based variations require active management and adjustment to optimize outcomes and mitigate risks.

- **Capital Requirements**: The standard Wheel Strategy requires substantial capital since it involves purchasing 100 shares of the underlying stock per option contract. The Credit Spreads variation reduces capital needs by capping potential losses, while the Ratio Spreads may involve higher capital compared to the Credit Spread version. Both the Credit Spread and the Ratio version require the capital to but 100 shares of the underlying stock if assigned.

- **Risk Potential:** The standard Wheel Strategy and the Ratio one carry high risk if the stock price drops significantly, while the Credit Spreads offers more defined risk profile.

- **Profit Expectations:** The standard Wheel offers steady but limited profits, with potentially lower profits if assigned. Credit Spreads provide moderate profits with defined risk, while Ratio Spreads can generate higher returns due to leveraged positions.

- **Pros and Cons:** The standard Wheel offers ease and consistency but has lower profit potential and protection. The credit and ratio spread variations introduce more complexity and management but provide opportunities for higher returns and better risk management.

UNLEASH THE POWER OF ADVANCED INCOME STRATEGIES

Aspect	Wheel Strategy	Wheel Strategy with Credit Spreads	Wheel Strategy with Ratio Spreads
Strategy Goal	Focus on consistent premium collection. Ideally, avoid assignment but accept it when it occurs. Premium is collected regardless of assignment status	Aim to collect premium while limiting risk with defined spreads. Focus on capital efficiency. Prepared to manage assignments with spreads	Collect premium with potential for larger returns. Accept risk of being assigned. Use ratio spreads to amplify profit potential
Expected Market Environment	Suitable for low to moderate volatility. Works best in a stable or slightly bullish market. Less effective in highly volatile or bearish markets	Best in stable or slightly volatile markets. Spreads offer some protection in mildly bearish markets. Works well in moderate volatility	Ideal for moderate to high volatility. Can be effective in various market conditions. Suitable for traders expecting a significant price movement
Expected Exit	Aim for stock price near the assigned strike price. High premium for covered calls when close to strike price. Simple exit if stock price stays favorable	Exit with profit if spread expires worthless or adjust to mitigate risk. Roll or adjust spreads based on stock movement and time decay	Prefer stock close to the short strikes to maximize profits. Adjust or roll spreads for better positioning. Complex multiple adjustments possible
Capital Requirements	High capital required for cash-secured puts and covered calls. Must be able to purchase 100 shares per contract	Lower capital requirement due to spread structure. Maximum loss is capped by the spread. In case of assignment, the capital requirement is the same as the standard Wheel	Capital requirement varies depending on spread width and ratio. Can involve higher capital than credit spreads but less than standard Wheel. In case of assignment, the capital requirement is the same as the standard Wheel
Risk Potential	High risk if the stock price drops significantly below the put strike. Potential for large losses if assigned and the stock continues to drop. Limited upside	Defined risk with limited downside due to spreads. Capped profits but less risk of catastrophic loss	High risk due to potential for significant losses if stock moves sharply against the position. Complex risk management. Requires strong knowledge of ratio spreads
Profit Potential	Consistent but limited profit potential. Profits mainly from premium collection. Assignment leads to lower potential profit	Moderate profit potential. Profits are capped but losses are limited. Suitable for conservative income generation	High profit potential due to ratio spreads. Potential for outsized returns. Profits can be significant if stock moves favorably
Overall Pros	Consistent premium collection. Simpler to execute and manage. Predictable income stream. Minimal complexity	More capital efficient than the standard Wheel. Defined risk with spreads. Enhanced risk management with limited downside	Higher potential returns due to ratio spreads. Profit from both assigned and unassigned positions. Can benefit from controlled leverage and increased premium collection
Overall Cons	Lower profit potential if assigned compared to more complex strategies. Less downside protection. Potentially worse breakeven point	Requires more active management and adjustments. Limited upside due to capped profits. Increased complexity and risk management needed. More involved strategy execution	Higher complexity with significant potential for adjustments. Risk of substantial losses if stock moves significantly. Requires strong understanding of options and ratio spreads. More time-intensive to manage effectively

Table 2 - Wheel Strategies - Comparison

CONCLUSION

HARNESSING THE POWER OF OPTION INCOME STRATEGIES

As we conclude our exploration of this volume, it's important to reflect on the most critical takeaways that will empower you on your journey to financial success. This eBook has equipped you with a thorough understanding of various strategies and techniques that can significantly enhance your trading endeavors. Here's a summary of the essential concepts and insights:

Key Takeaways

- **Income Generation**:
    - **Advanced Income Strategies:** Deep understanding of a range of options strategies, each with unique approaches to managing risk and generating income. Techniques like vertical spreads and iron condors provide structured ways to profit from different market conditions, while strategies such as short strangles and short straddles focus on exploiting market stability.
    - **Stock Repair Strategy:** A methodical approach aiming to recover from stock losses using options.

TOOLS AND MARKET STRATEGIES FOR A THRIVING OPTIONS BUSINESS

- **The Wheel Strategy:** A cyclical trading approach where traders sell puts and calls to generate income. It combines income collection with stock acquisition, offering a consistent way to profit from both option premiums and stock movements.
- **LEAPS Options:** LEAPS (Long-term Equity Anticipation Securities) offer a way to gain long-term exposure with lower capital outlay compared to buying stocks outright. They can be used to leverage long-term market views efficiently.
- **Alternative Wheel Strategies:** Incorporate credit and ratio spreads into the Wheel Strategy to refine risk management and enhance potential returns. These variations offer more nuanced approaches to managing trades and capital.

The Value of Income Strategies

The advanced income strategies explored in the second volume of The Option Trader's Income Blueprint introduce sophisticated techniques to elevate your trading outcomes. This volume delves into refined approaches such as vertical credit spreads, iron condors, and ratio spreads, which provide more nuanced ways to manage risk and maximize income. By mastering these strategies, including the Wheel Strategy with credit and ratio spreads, you can enhance your capital efficiency, generate consistent returns, and adapt to varying market conditions. These advanced methods are designed to offer both stability and potential for higher gains, enabling you to navigate the complexities of options trading with greater precision and confidence. With the knowledge you've gained from this book, you are now equipped to take action. Start by applying the concepts and techniques to set up a more advanced option income portfolio.

Here are a few general steps to get started:

- **Start Small**: Begin with small trades and gradually increase your position size as you gain experience and confidence. Avoid putting too much capital at risk in the early stages.
- **Assess Your Portfolio**: Evaluate your current investments and identify opportunities to apply the covered call and cash-secured put strategies.
- **Choose Appropriate Strategies**: Select strategies that align with your market outlook and risk tolerance, focusing on the

foundational techniques and more advanced strategies discussed in this volume.
- **Review and Adjust**: Regularly monitor your trades and portfolio, adjusting as necessary based on market conditions.
- **Commit to Continuous Learning**: While this book provides a strong foundation, remember that options trading is a complex field. Stay informed about market developments and consider exploring the other volumes in this series to deepen your knowledge and refine your strategies.
- **Risk Management**: Prioritize risk management in every trade. Define your maximum acceptable loss and avoid chasing losses. Protecting your capital should always be your top priority.
- **Patience and Discipline**: Successful options trading requires patience and discipline. Stick to your trading plan, avoid impulsive decisions, and don't let emotions drive your trades.

This second volume is an essential progression in your options trading journey. The advanced strategies and insights covered here will enhance your trading skills and deepen your understanding of complex income techniques. Building on the foundational knowledge from the first volume, this book equips you with sophisticated methods to refine your approach and optimize your financial outcomes.

As you implement these advanced strategies, remember that mastering options trading is an ongoing process. Each subsequent volume in this series will further expand your expertise, offering new perspectives and strategies to achieve even greater success. Embrace the opportunities presented, apply these advanced concepts with precision, and continue your journey with the confidence that you are well-equipped to reach your financial goals. The path to mastery continues with the next volume, where more advanced risk management techniques await.

GLOSSARY

A

Alpha: Alpha measures the excess return of an investment relative to the return predicted by the CAPM or another benchmark. It reflects the performance of an asset or portfolio after accounting for market-related risks. A positive alpha indicates that the investment has outperformed its expected return, suggesting effective management or superior asset selection.

American Option: An American option is an options contract that can be exercised at any time before or on the expiration date. This flexibility allows the holder to take advantage of favorable movements in the underlying asset's price at any point during the life of the option. American options are commonly used for stocks and ETFs, providing opportunities for early exercise, such as when a stock pays a dividend.

Anchoring: Anchoring is a cognitive bias where an individual relies too heavily on the first piece of information encountered when making decisions. In trading, this can affect how investors assess the value of assets or set price targets.

Asset Class: An asset class is a category of financial assets with similar characteristics, such as stocks, bonds, commodities, or real estate. Different asset classes typically have different risk and return profiles.

At the Money (ATM): An option is "at the money" when the underlying asset's price is equal to the option's strike price. In this case, the option has no intrinsic value but may still have time value.

Autocorrelation Function (ACF): The Autocorrelation Function (ACF) measures the correlation between a time series and a lagged version of itself. It quantifies how current values of the series are related to past values at different time lags. This function is crucial for identifying patterns and seasonality in time series data. For example, in stock price analysis, a significant autocorrelation at a lag of 12 months might indicate annual seasonal effects.

B

Beta: Beta is a measure of an asset's sensitivity to market movements, capturing its systematic risk. It quantifies how much an asset's returns are expected to change in response to market fluctuations. A beta of 1 implies that the asset moves with the market, while a beta greater or less than 1 indicates higher or lower volatility relative to the market, respectively.

Bid-Ask Spread: The bid-ask spread is the difference between the highest price a buyer is willing to pay (bid) and the lowest price a seller is willing to accept (ask) for a security. It represents the cost of liquidity in the market. A narrower spread indicates a more liquid market, while a wider spread suggests lower liquidity and higher transaction costs.

Binomial Model: The binomial model is an option pricing model that uses a tree of possible future prices for the underlying asset to estimate the option's value. It accounts for multiple time periods and possible outcomes.

Black-Litterman Model: The Black-Litterman model is an asset allocation model that combines market equilibrium with investor views to generate more stable and diversified portfolios. It is used to improve the robustness of portfolio construction.

Black-Scholes Model: The Black-Scholes model is a mathematical model used to estimate the fair value of options. It considers factors such as the underlying asset's price, volatility, time to expiration, and interest rates to calculate the option's price.

Blue-Chip Stock: A blue-chip stock is a stock of a large, well-established, and financially stable company with a history of reliable earnings and dividend payments. Blue-chip stocks are typically considered low-risk investments.

Bollinger Bands: Bollinger Bands are technical analysis tools that plot an asset's price within bands based on its moving average and standard deviation. They are used to assess volatility and identify potential reversal points.

Book Value per Share: Book value per share is calculated by dividing a company's total equity by the number of outstanding shares. It represents the value of a company's net assets on a per-share basis and is used as a measure of intrinsic value. Investors use it to assess whether a stock is under- or overvalued relative to its book value.

Breakeven Point: The breakeven point is the underlying asset price at which the options strategy results in neither profit nor loss. It is calculated by factoring in the premiums received or paid.

Broker: A broker is a financial intermediary that facilitates the buying and selling of financial instruments, such as stocks, bonds, and options, on behalf of clients. Brokers may also provide advice and research services.

Buying Power: Buying power is the total amount of capital available to a trader for opening new positions, considering both cash and margin. It determines the maximum size of trades that can be executed.

C

Call: A call option grants the holder the right to buy an underlying asset at a specified strike price within a specified period. The seller of the call option has the obligation to sell the asset if the buyer exercises the option.

Call Ratio Spread: A call ratio spread involves buying a certain number of call options and selling a larger number of call options with the same expiration date but a different strike price. It is a neutral to bullish strategy.

Capital Asset Pricing Model (CAPM): The Capital Asset Pricing Model (CAPM) is a financial model that describes the relationship between systematic risk and expected return for assets, particularly stocks. It is used to estimate the cost of equity.

Capital Expenditures (CapEx): CapEx refers to the funds used by a company to acquire, upgrade, or maintain physical assets such as property, plant, and equipment. CapEx is essential for sustaining and growing a company's operations but represents a significant cash outflow. Analysts monitor CapEx to assess a company's investment in its future growth and its impact on free cash flow.

Capital Market Line (CML): The Capital Market Line (CML) represents the risk-return tradeoff in a market where all investors have identical expectations and can borrow or lend at the risk-free rate. It shows the optimal portfolio of risky assets combined with the risk-free asset.

Capital Requirement: Capital requirement refers to the amount of funds that must be reserved to cover the potential obligations of an options strategy, such as the cost of buying the underlying asset or margin requirements.

Capital Reserve: A capital reserve is a portion of a trader's capital set aside to cover potential losses. It provides a financial cushion for the trader.

Cash-Secured Put: A cash-secured put involves selling a put option while holding enough cash to purchase the underlying asset if the option is exercised. This strategy generates income from the premium while being prepared to buy the asset at the strike price.

Cash Settlement: Cash settlement is a method of settling an options contract by paying the cash difference between the strike price and the market price of the underlying asset, rather than delivering the physical asset. This is common in index options, where it is impractical to deliver the underlying assets. Upon exercise, the option holder receives a cash amount equal to the profit they would have made if the option were physically settled.

Central Banks: Central banks are national financial institutions responsible for managing a country's monetary policy, regulating banks, and maintaining financial stability. They influence interest rates, control inflation, and implement policies to stabilize the economy. Notable examples include the Federal Reserve (Fed) in the United States and the European Central Bank (ECB) in the Eurozone.

Collar: A collar is an options strategy that involves holding a long position in an asset, buying a protective put, and selling a covered call. It limits both the upside and downside potential, providing a balanced risk-reward profile.

Commodity: A commodity is a raw material or primary agricultural product that can be bought and sold, such as oil, gold, or wheat. Commodities are traded on specialized markets and are subject to supply and demand fluctuations.

Commodity Futures Trading (CFT): Commodity Futures Trading (CFT) involves buying and selling futures contracts for commodities such as oil, gold, or agricultural products. Futures contracts are agreements to buy or sell a commodity at a predetermined price on a specified future date. This trading helps manage price risk and speculate on future price movements.

Confidence Interval: A confidence interval is a range of values derived from a data set that is likely to contain the true population parameter with a specified level of confidence, such as 95%.

Consumer Confidence Index (CCI): The Consumer Confidence Index (CCI) measures the degree of optimism that consumers feel about the overall state of the economy and their personal financial situation. It is a leading economic indicator that can predict consumer spending patterns, which in turn affects economic growth. A rising CCI typically signals increased consumer spending and economic expansion.

Consumer Price Index (CPI): The Consumer Price Index (CPI) tracks changes in the average prices paid by consumers for a basket of goods and services over time. It is a key indicator of inflation, reflecting the cost of living and purchasing power. Central banks use CPI to adjust monetary policy to maintain price stability.

Correlation: Correlation is a statistical measure that indicates the degree to which two assets move in relation to each other. A positive correlation means they move in the same direction, while a negative correlation means they move in opposite directions.

Correlation Matrix: A correlation matrix is a table showing the correlation coefficients between multiple assets. It helps in understanding the relationships between different assets and is used in portfolio optimization.

Covariance: Covariance is a measure of how two variables change together. In finance, it is used to assess how the returns of two assets move relative to each other, helping in portfolio diversification.

Covered Call: A covered call strategy involves holding a long position in an underlying asset and selling a call option on the same asset. It generates income from the option premium while potentially capping the upside.

Credit Risk: Credit risk is the risk of loss arising from a borrower or counterparty's failure to meet their contractual obligations. It is a key consideration in lending and derivatives markets.

Cumulative Distribution Function (CDF): The Cumulative Distribution Function (CDF) of a random variable X is a function $F_X(x)$ that describes the probability that X will take a value less than or equal to x.

Cyclical Sectors: Cyclical sectors include industries that are highly sensitive to economic cycles, with performance closely tied to the overall health of the economy. Companies in these sectors, such as consumer discretionary, industrials, materials, financials, and real estate, tend to perform well during economic expansions and suffer during recessions.

D

Debt to Equity (D/E) Ratio: The D/E ratio is a financial leverage metric that compares a company's total debt to its shareholders' equity. It indicates the proportion of financing that comes from debt versus equity. A higher D/E ratio suggests greater financial risk, as the company relies more on borrowed funds. Conversely, a lower ratio indicates a more conservative capital structure.

Defensive Sectors: Defensive sectors consist of industries that are less sensitive to economic cycles and tend to perform relatively well during economic downturns. These sectors, such as consumer staples, healthcare, and utilities, provide essential goods and services that remain in demand regardless of economic conditions.

Delta: Delta measures the sensitivity of an option's price to changes in the price of the underlying asset. It ranges from 0 to 1 for calls and from 0 to -1 for puts, indicating the probability of the option being in the money at expiration.

Delta Hedging: Delta hedging is a risk management strategy used in options trading that involves adjusting the position in the underlying asset to offset changes in the option's delta. Delta represents the sensitivity of an option's price to changes in the price of the underlying asset. By frequently adjusting the position, the trader aims to maintain a delta-neutral portfolio, reducing exposure to price movements in the underlying asset.

Distribution: Distribution in finance and statistics refers to the way values, such as returns, prices, or other data points, are spread or dispersed over a range. In the context of financial markets, distribution often describes how the returns of an asset are spread across different possible outcomes, typically visualized in a histogram or a probability density function.

Diversification (Portfolio): Diversification is the practice of spreading investments across various asset classes, sectors, or instruments to reduce risk. A diversified portfolio is less likely to suffer large losses from the poor performance of a single asset.

Dividend: A dividend is a portion of a company's earnings distributed to shareholders, typically in the form of cash or additional shares. Dividends are a key component of total return for investors and can signal a company's financial health and stability. The dividend yield, calculated as the annual dividend per share divided by the share price, indicates the income generated by holding the stock.

Dividend Yield: Dividend yield is a financial ratio that indicates the annual dividend income received from a stock relative to its current price. It is a measure of the income generated from an investment in a stock.

Dividend-Paying Stock: A dividend-paying stock is a stock of a company that regularly distributes a portion of its earnings to shareholders in the form of dividends. These stocks are often favored by income-focused investors.

Double Down: Double down is an aggressive trading strategy where a trader increases their position size in a losing trade to average down the entry price, aiming for a larger profit when the market reverses.

Downside Deviation: Downside deviation is a measure of the variability of returns that fall below a specified threshold, typically the risk-free rate or a target return. Unlike standard deviation, which considers all volatility, downside deviation focuses only on negative returns. It is used in performance evaluation and risk management to assess the extent of potential losses and the likelihood of not meeting investment objectives.

Drawdown: Drawdown is the peak-to-trough decline in the value of a trading account or investment. It measures the amount of loss before a new peak is achieved, reflecting the risk of a trading strategy.

E

Earnings per Share (EPS): EPS measures a company's profitability by dividing its net income by the number of outstanding shares. It represents the portion of a company's profit allocated to each share of stock and is a key indicator of financial performance. Higher EPS typically indicates greater profitability and is often used to compare companies within the same industry.

Economic Cycle: The Economic Cycle refers to the natural rise and fall of economic growth over time. It includes four phases: Expansion (increasing economic activity), Peak (the height of economic activity), Contraction (a decline in economic activity), and Trough (the lowest point of economic activity before recovery begins).

Efficient Frontier: The efficient frontier is a line on a risk-return graph representing the set of optimal portfolios that offer the highest expected return for a given level of risk. Portfolios on the efficient frontier are considered well-diversified.

Equity: Equity represents ownership in a company, typically in the form of stocks. It entitles the holder to a share of the company's assets and earnings and may also include voting rights.

ETF (Exchange-Traded Fund): An ETF is a type of investment fund that is traded on stock exchanges, much like stocks. It holds a collection of assets, such as stocks, bonds, or commodities, and allows investors to diversify their holdings.

European Central Bank (ECB): The European Central Bank (ECB) is the central bank for the Eurozone, responsible for monetary policy within the Euro area. Its main objectives include maintaining price stability, managing interest rates, and regulating financial institutions to ensure economic stability.

European Option: A European option is a type of options contract that can only be exercised on its expiration date. Unlike American options, which can be exercised at any time before expiration, European options restrict the exercise of the option to a single point in time. These options are often used in financial markets for index options and other instruments where early exercise is not typically necessary.

European Securities and Markets Authority (ESMA): The European Securities and Markets Authority (ESMA) is a European Union regulatory agency responsible for improving the functioning of financial markets and enhancing investor protection. It oversees securities markets, ensures transparency, and enforces regulations across the EU.

Event Risk: Event risk arises from unforeseen events such as geopolitical tensions, economic crises, or corporate scandals that can dramatically impact financial markets, leading to sharp movements in asset prices.

Expectancy: Expectancy refers to the expected average outcome of a trading strategy over time, calculated by considering both the probability of success and the potential rewards and losses.

Expected Loss: Expected loss is the anticipated average loss from a trading strategy, considering the likelihood of losing trades and the size of those losses. It is a key metric in risk management.

F

Federal Open Market Committee (FOMC): The Federal Open Market Committee (FOMC) is a component of the Federal Reserve that oversees open market operations and sets monetary policy. It meets regularly to review economic conditions and make decisions on interest rates and other monetary policies to influence economic growth and inflation.

Federal Reserve (FED): The Federal Reserve, or Fed, is the central banking system of the United States. It is responsible for conducting monetary policy, supervising and regulating banks, maintaining financial stability, and providing financial services. It influences interest rates and money supply to promote economic stability.

Financial Services Authority (FSA): The Financial Services Authority (FSA) was a regulatory body in the UK responsible for regulating financial services and markets. It was replaced by the Financial Conduct Authority (FCA) and the Prudential Regulation Authority (PRA) in 2013. It aimed to protect consumers, maintain market integrity, and promote competition.

FOMO (Fear of Missing Out): FOMO is a psychological phenomenon where traders or investors feel compelled to enter a trade or investment out of fear of missing out on potential profits. It can lead to impulsive and irrational decision-making.

Fourier Analysis: Fourier Analysis is a mathematical method used to analyze and decompose time series data into its frequency components. By transforming a time series from the time domain to the frequency domain, Fourier Analysis helps identify cyclical patterns and periodicities in the data.

Free Cash Flow (FCF): FCF represents the cash generated by a company after accounting for capital expenditures necessary to maintain or expand its asset base. It is a key indicator of financial flexibility and the ability to generate shareholder value. Positive FCF allows a company to invest in growth, pay dividends, reduce debt, or repurchase shares.

G

Gamma: Gamma measures the rate of change of delta with respect to changes in the underlying asset's price. It reflects the convexity of the option's price and indicates the stability of the delta.

Gamma Scalping: Gamma scalping is a dynamic hedging strategy used in options trading to manage the gamma risk of an options position. Gamma measures the rate of change in an option's delta as the underlying asset price moves. By frequently adjusting the position in the underlying asset, traders aim to maintain a delta-neutral position and capture profits from price movements while managing the risks associated with gamma exposure.

Gross Domestic Product (GDP): Gross Domestic Product (GDP) measures the total value of goods and services produced within a country's borders over a specific period. It is a key indicator of economic performance and growth. Rising GDP typically indicates economic expansion, while falling GDP may signal a recession.

Growth Stock: A growth stock is a stock of a company expected to grow at an above-average rate compared to other companies in the market. Growth stocks typically do not pay dividends, as profits are reinvested into the company.

H

Hedging: Hedging is a risk management strategy used to offset potential losses in an investment by taking an opposing position in a related asset, such as using options to protect against adverse price movements in a stock.

Historical Distribution: Historical distribution refers to the frequency distribution of past returns or prices of an asset. It helps in understanding the asset's historical behavior and estimating future performance.

Historical Volatility: Historical volatility measures the past price fluctuations of an asset over a specific period. It is calculated as the standard deviation of returns and provides insight into the asset's past price behavior.

I

Implied Volatility: Implied volatility is a forward-looking measure derived from the option's market price. It reflects the market's expectations of future price fluctuations of the underlying asset.

Implied Volatility Percentile (IV Percentile): Implied Volatility Percentile measures the percentage of time that the implied volatility has been below the current level over a specific period, typically a year. A higher percentile indicates relatively high implied volatility.

Implied Volatility Rank (IV Rank): Implied Volatility Rank compares the current implied volatility of an asset to its range over a specific period, usually a year. It indicates whether the current IV is high or low relative to its historical values.

In the Money (ITM): An option is "in the money" when exercising it would lead to a positive cash flow. For a call option, this means the underlying asset's price is above the strike price. For a put option, it means the asset's price is below the strike price.

Index: An index is a statistical measure that tracks the performance of a group of assets, such as stocks or bonds, representing a specific market or sector. Indices are used as benchmarks for portfolio performance.

Interest Cost: Interest cost is the expense incurred from borrowing funds to finance a leveraged position. It reduces the net return on leveraged trades and must be considered in margin trading.

Intrinsic Value: Intrinsic value is the value of an option if it were exercised immediately. It is the difference between the underlying asset's price and the option's strike price, provided it is favorable to the option holder.

Inverted Strangle: An inverted strangle involves selling an in-the-money call and put, with the put having a higher strike price than the call.

Iron Butterfly: Iron Butterfly is risk-defined options strategy that involves four options contracts, typically using the same expiration date. The strategy combines elements of both a straddle (short) and a strangle (long) and is designed to profit from low volatility and minimal movement in the underlying asset's price.

Iron Condor: An iron condor is an options strategy that involves selling an out-of-the-money call and put, while simultaneously buying a further out-of-the-money call and put. It is a neutral strategy that profits from low volatility.

K

Kelly Criterion: The Kelly Criterion is a mathematical formula used to determine the optimal size of a series of bets or trades to maximize long-term growth while managing risk. It is based on the probability of success and the ratio of wins to losses.

L

Large-Cap: Large-cap stocks refer to shares of companies with a market capitalization typically above $10 billion. These companies are often well-established, with stable revenue streams and a significant presence in their industries. Large-cap stocks are generally considered less volatile and offer more predictable returns than smaller companies.

LEAPS Option (Long-Term Equity Anticipation Security): LEAPS are long-term options, typically with expiration dates longer than one year, that provide extended exposure to the underlying asset. They are used for long-term speculation or hedging.

Leverage: Leverage involves using borrowed funds or margin to increase the potential return of an investment. It amplifies both profits and losses, making it a high-risk, high-reward strategy.

Liabilities: Total liabilities encompass all financial obligations a company owes to external parties, including short-term and long-term debt, accounts payable, and other liabilities. It is a key component of a company's balance sheet and is used in conjunction with total assets to assess financial stability and leverage.

Liquidity: Liquidity refers to the ease with which an asset can be bought or sold in the market without affecting its price. High liquidity ensures efficient market functioning and tighter bid-ask spreads.

Liquidity Risk: Liquidity risk is the risk that an asset cannot be bought or sold quickly enough in the market without significantly affecting its price, leading to potential losses or the inability to execute trades.

Loss Aversion: Loss aversion is a behavioral finance concept that describes the tendency of individuals to prefer avoiding losses rather than acquiring equivalent gains. It can lead to suboptimal decision-making in trading.

M

MACD (Moving Average Convergence Divergence): MACD is a momentum indicator that shows the relationship between two moving averages of an asset's price. It helps identify trends, potential buy/sell signals, and changes in momentum.

Manufacturing Purchasing Managers' Index (PMI): The Manufacturing Purchasing Managers' Index (PMI) is an economic indicator derived from surveys of manufacturing executives. It measures the health of the manufacturing sector, including factors such as production levels, new orders, and employment. A PMI above 50 indicates expansion, while below 50 indicates contraction.

Margin Call: A margin call occurs when a trader's account equity falls below the required margin level, prompting the broker to demand additional funds or the liquidation of positions to restore the margin balance.

Margin Requirement: Margin requirement refers to the minimum amount of equity that must be maintained in a margin account when holding leveraged positions. It is set by the broker or regulatory bodies and varies by asset type.

Market Cap: Market capitalization, or market cap, is the total value of a company's outstanding shares of stock. It is calculated by multiplying the current stock price by the total number of outstanding shares. Market cap is used to classify companies into different categories, such as large-cap, mid-cap, and small-cap, which helps investors assess a company's size and market value.

Market Risk: Market risk refers to the potential for losses due to factors that affect the overall performance of financial markets, such as economic changes, interest rates, and geopolitical events.

Mean: The mean is the average of a data set, calculated by summing all the values and dividing by the number of observations. It is a measure of central tendency.

Median: The median is the middle value in a data set when the values are arranged in ascending or descending order. It represents the 50th percentile and is less affected by outliers than the mean.

Micro-Cap: Micro-cap stocks refer to companies with a market capitalization between approximately 50 million and 300 million. These stocks are often associated with higher risk and volatility due to their smaller size and limited liquidity, but they can offer significant growth potential.

Mid-Cap: Mid-cap stocks are shares of companies with a market capitalization ranging from approximately 2 billion to 10 billion. These companies are usually in a growth phase, offering a balance between stability and potential for higher returns. Mid-cap stocks can be more volatile than large-cap stocks but often provide greater growth opportunities.

Mode: The mode is the value that appears most frequently in a data set. It is a measure of central tendency that indicates the most common observation.

Modern Portfolio Theory (MPT): Modern Portfolio Theory (MPT) is an investment framework that emphasizes the importance of diversification to optimize portfolio returns for a given level of risk. It introduces the concept of the efficient frontier.

Monte Carlo Simulation: Monte Carlo Simulation is a statistical technique that uses random sampling to model the probability of different outcomes in a complex system. It is used in finance to estimate the range of potential future returns.

Moving Averages: Moving Averages are statistical tools used to smooth out fluctuations in time series data and identify trends. They are calculated by averaging data points over a specific period. Common types include Simple Moving Averages (SMA) and Exponential Moving Averages (EMA), each serving different purposes in trend analysis.

N

Nano-Cap: Nano-cap stocks are the smallest publicly traded companies, with market capitalizations typically below $50 million. These stocks are highly speculative and volatile, with limited liquidity, making them risky investments but potentially rewarding for those seeking high-risk, high-reward opportunities.

Non-Farm Payrolls (NFP): Non-Farm Payrolls (NFP) refer to the number of jobs added or lost in the U.S. economy, excluding farm workers, government employees, and some other sectors. It is a key monthly indicator of economic health and employment trends, influencing market expectations and central bank policies.

Normal Distribution: A normal distribution is a statistical distribution where data points are symmetrically distributed around the mean, forming a bell-shaped curve. It is used in finance to model returns and assess probabilities.

O

Open Interest: Open interest refers to the total number of outstanding derivative contracts, such as options or futures, that have not been settled. It is a measure of market activity and liquidity, with higher open interest indicating a more active and liquid market. Open interest is used to gauge the strength of a market trend and potential price movements.

Operating Cash Flow (OCF): OCF measures the cash generated by a company's core operating activities, excluding capital expenditures. It reflects the company's ability to generate sufficient cash flow to sustain operations and fund day-to-day activities. OCF is a critical indicator of a company's financial health and operational efficiency.

Operational Risk: Operational risk involves losses resulting from failures in internal processes, systems, or controls. This includes technical issues, human errors, or system outages that can impact trading execution and strategy implementation.

Option: An option is a financial derivative that gives the holder the right, but not the obligation, to buy (call) or sell (put) an underlying asset at a specified strike price before or on a specified expiration date. Options are used for hedging, speculation, and income generation.

Option Adjustments: Option adjustments involve modifying an existing options position to manage risk, improve returns, or respond to market conditions. Adjustments may include rolling, adding or closing positions.

Option Expiration Date: The option expiration date is the last date on which the option can be exercised. After this date, the option expires and becomes worthless if not exercised.

Option Premium: The option premium is the price paid by the buyer to the seller for the rights conferred by the option. It consists of the intrinsic value and the time value of the option.

Option Time Value: Option time value represents the portion of the option premium that exceeds its intrinsic value. It reflects the potential for the option to gain value before expiration due to market movements.

Out of the Money (OTM): An option is "out of the money" when exercising it would not be profitable. For a call option, this occurs when the underlying asset's price is below the strike price. For a put option, it happens when the asset's price is above the strike price.

P

Paper Trading: Paper trading involves simulated trading in a risk-free environment using virtual money. It allows traders to practice strategies and gain experience without risking real capital.

Payoff: The payoff is the profit or loss realized from holding an option at expiration or after exercising it. It depends on the difference between the strike price and the underlying asset's market price.

Penny Stocks: Penny stocks refer to shares of small, often speculative companies that trade at low prices, typically under $5 per share. These stocks are highly volatile and risky, with limited liquidity and a higher likelihood of price manipulation, but they can offer substantial returns if the company succeeds.

Percentile: A percentile is a measure used to indicate the value below which a given percentage of observations fall in a data set. It is used in statistical analysis to compare relative standing.

Personal Consumption Expenditure (PCE): Personal Consumption Expenditure (PCE) measures the changes in the prices of goods and services consumed by households. It is a key indicator of inflation and consumer spending. The Federal Reserve closely monitors the PCE index to guide monetary policy decisions.

Physical Settlement: Physical settlement refers to the process of fulfilling an options contract by delivering the actual underlying asset. When an option is exercised, the seller (writer) of the option must deliver the physical asset, such as stocks, bonds, or commodities, to the buyer. For example, if a call option on a stock is exercised, the seller must deliver the specified number of shares to the buyer at the agreed-upon strike price.

Position Sizing: Position sizing is the process of determining how much capital to allocate to a single trade based on the risk involved and the overall trading strategy. Proper position sizing helps manage risk by ensuring that no single trade can significantly impact the portfolio.

Post-Modern Portfolio Theory (PMPT): Post-Modern Portfolio Theory (PMPT) is an extension of MPT that focuses on downside risk and investor preferences. It incorporates measures like the Sortino ratio to better reflect investor concerns about losses.

Potential Loss: Potential loss refers to the possible loss that can occur from an options strategy.

Pre-Market / After-Hours Trading: Pre-Market and After-Hours Trading refer to the trading of securities outside the regular market hours. Pre-Market Trading occurs before the market opens, while After-Hours Trading happens after the market closes. These sessions allow investors to react to news and events that occur outside normal trading hours.

Price to Book (P/B) Ratio: The P/B ratio compares a company's market value to its book value, calculated as the market price per share divided by the book value per share. It reflects how much investors are willing to pay for each dollar of net assets. A P/B ratio greater than 1 suggests that the market values the company more than its book value, often due to expectations of future growth.

Price to Earnings (P/E) Ratio: The P/E ratio is a valuation metric that compares a company's current share price to its earnings per share (EPS). It indicates how much investors are willing to pay for each dollar of earnings. A high P/E ratio may suggest that the stock is overvalued or that investors expect high growth in the future, while a low P/E ratio may indicate undervaluation.

Probability Density Function (PDF): The Probability Density Function (PDF) of a continuous random variable X is a function $f_X(x)$ that describes the likelihood of X taking a specific value x.

Probability of Touching: The probability of touching refers to the likelihood that the underlying asset's price will reach or exceed a specific strike price at least once during the option's life. It is generally higher than the probability of the option being in the money at expiration.

Put: A put option gives the holder the right to sell an underlying asset at a predetermined strike price within a specified timeframe. The seller of the put option is obliged to purchase the asset if the option is exercised.

Put Ratio Spread: A put ratio spread involves buying a certain number of put options and selling a larger number of put options with the same expiration date but a different strike price. It is a neutral to bearish strategy.

R

Recency Bias: Recency bias is a cognitive bias where individuals give undue weight to recent events or experiences when making decisions. In trading, this can lead to overestimating the importance of short-term market movements.

Regression Analysis with Seasonal Dummies: Regression Analysis with Seasonal Dummies involves incorporating dummy variables representing different seasons or months into a regression model. This technique helps quantify and control for seasonal effects on a time series, improving the accuracy of forecasts and understanding seasonal impacts on the dependent variable.

Retail Sales: Retail Sales measure the total receipts of retail stores, reflecting consumer spending patterns. It is a key economic indicator that provides insights into consumer confidence and economic health. An increase in retail sales suggests higher consumer spending and economic growth.

Return (Daily): Daily return is the percentage change in the value of an asset from one day to the next. It is a key metric for measuring short-term performance and calculating volatility.

Rho: Rho measures the sensitivity of an option's price to changes in interest rates. It indicates how much the option's price will change for a 1% change in interest rates.

Risk Parity: Risk parity is a portfolio construction strategy that allocates capital based on the risk contribution of each asset, rather than allocating based on expected returns or capital alone. The goal is to equalize the risk across different asset classes, achieving a more balanced and diversified portfolio. This method often involves leveraging lower-risk assets to equalize risk exposure across the portfolio.

Rolling (Option) Up/Down/Out: Rolling an option involves closing an existing position and opening a new one with a different strike price or expiration date. Rolling up or down adjusts the strike price, while rolling out extends the expiration date.

S

Seasonal Autoregressive Integrated Moving Average (SARIMA): Seasonal Autoregressive Integrated Moving Average (SARIMA) is a time series forecasting model that extends the ARIMA model by including seasonal components. It accounts for both non-seasonal and seasonal patterns in data, making it suitable for forecasting with strong seasonal effects.

Seasonal Decomposition of Time Series by LOESS (STL): Seasonal Decomposition of Time Series by LOESS (STL) is a method for decomposing a time series into its trend, seasonal, and residual components using locally weighted regression (LOESS). STL is flexible and can handle any type of seasonality and trend, providing a robust decomposition of the time series.

Seasonal Subseries Plot: A Seasonal Subseries Plot is a graphical tool used to visualize seasonal patterns within a time series. It displays data for each season (e.g., month) across multiple years in separate subplots. This visualization helps identify recurring seasonal trends and variations.

Securities and Exchange Commission (SEC): The Securities and Exchange Commission (SEC) is the U.S. regulatory agency responsible for overseeing securities markets and protecting investors. It enforces federal securities laws, regulates stock exchanges, and ensures fair and transparent trading practices.

Sector: An economic sector refers to a large segment of the economy that is made up of companies and industries with similar business activities. Sectors are often used to categorize companies for investment analysis. Common sectors include Technology, Healthcare, Financials, Energy, and Consumer Discretionary.

Sensitive Sectors: Sensitive sectors include industries that have moderate correlations with business cycles. These sectors, such as technology, energy, and communication services, are influenced by economic conditions but may not be as directly tied to the business cycle as cyclical sectors

Sensitivity Analysis: Sensitivity analysis in option trading involves evaluating how the price or risk metrics of an option or a portfolio of options respond to changes in underlying factors such as the price of the underlying asset, implied volatility, interest rates, or time to expiration.

Sharpe Ratio: The Sharpe Ratio measures the risk-adjusted return of an investment by comparing the excess return (over the risk-free rate) to its standard deviation. It is a key metric for evaluating the performance of a portfolio, with a higher Sharpe Ratio indicating better risk-adjusted returns. The ratio helps investors assess whether an investment's returns justify its risk.

Short Selling: Short selling involves selling an asset that the seller does not own, typically by borrowing it, with the intention of buying it back later at a lower price to make a profit.

Short Straddle: A short straddle involves selling both a call and a put option at the same strike price and expiration date. The strategy profits from low volatility and the expectation that the underlying asset will remain at or near the strike price.

Short Strangle: A short strangle involves selling an out-of-the-money call and put with the same expiration date. The strategy profits from low volatility and the expectation that the underlying asset will remain within a certain price range.

Simple Moving Average (SMA): A Simple Moving Average (SMA) is a technical analysis tool used to smooth out price data by creating a constantly updated average price over a specified period. The SMA is calculated by adding the closing prices of an asset over a set number of periods and then dividing the total by the number of periods.

Small-Cap: Small-cap stocks are shares of companies with a market capitalization between approximately 300 million and 2 billion. These companies are typically in the early stages of growth and can offer high potential returns but also come with increased risk and volatility.

Sortino Ratio: The Sortino Ratio is a variation of the Sharpe Ratio that focuses on downside risk by considering only the standard deviation of negative returns. It measures the risk-adjusted return relative to a target or minimum acceptable return, providing a more accurate assessment of performance for investments with asymmetric return distributions or significant downside risks.

Standard Deviation: Standard deviation is a statistical measure of the dispersion of returns around the mean. It quantifies the level of risk or volatility of an asset's price.

Stock: A stock represents ownership in a corporation and constitutes a claim on part of the company's assets and earnings. Stocks are traded on stock exchanges and are a fundamental component of investment portfolios.

Stock Repair Strategy: The stock repair strategy involves using options to reduce the break-even point on a losing stock position without additional capital investment. Typically, this is done by buying and selling call options to offset losses.

Stop Loss: A stop-loss is an order placed to sell a security when it reaches a certain price level, used to limit potential losses in a position. It is a key tool in risk management.

Stress Testing: Stress testing in option trading is the process of assessing how an option or portfolio of options would perform under extreme or adverse market conditions. This involves simulating various scenarios, such as significant price movements in the underlying asset, drastic changes in implied volatility, or sudden shifts in interest rates. The goal of stress testing is to identify potential vulnerabilities and to evaluate the potential impact on profitability and risk exposure.

Strike Price: The strike price is the price at which the holder of an option can buy (call) or sell (put) the underlying asset. It is a key determinant in the option's value and the decision to exercise.

Symmetry (Distribution): Distribution symmetry refers to the degree to which the values in a data set are evenly distributed around the mean. A perfectly symmetric distribution has equal values on both sides of the mean.

T

Tail Risk: Tail risk refers to the probability of rare, extreme events occurring that could cause significant losses in a portfolio. These events fall in the "tails" of the normal distribution curve of returns, hence the name. Managing tail risk often involves strategies such as buying options or other derivatives that increase in value during extreme market movements.

Theta: Theta represents the rate of time decay of an option. It quantifies how much the option's price decreases as the expiration date approaches, all else being equal.

Ticker: A ticker is a unique symbol or series of letters assigned to a publicly traded asset, such as a stock or ETF, to identify it on an exchange. Tickers are used to track prices and trades in the financial markets.

Time Decay (Theta): Time decay, measured by the option's theta, refers to the gradual decrease in the value of an option as it approaches its expiration date. It reflects the diminishing time value of the option.

Trading Plan: A trading plan is a documented set of rules and guidelines that a trader follows when executing trades. It includes criteria for entering and exiting trades, risk management strategies, and performance evaluation.

Transaction Costs: Transaction costs are expenses incurred when buying or selling securities. These costs include broker commissions, bid-ask spreads, and other fees associated with trading. Transaction costs can significantly impact investment returns, particularly for high-frequency trading strategies, and must be considered when evaluating the overall profitability of trades.

U

Underlying Asset (of an Option): The underlying asset is the financial instrument (e.g., stock, index, ETF) on which an option contract is based. The value and performance of the option are directly tied to the underlying asset.

Unemployment: Unemployment measures the percentage of the labor force that is actively seeking employment but is unable to find work. It is a critical economic indicator that reflects the health of the labor market and overall economic conditions. High unemployment rates can signal economic distress, while low rates typically indicate a robust job market.

V

Value at Risk (VaR): Value at Risk (VaR) is a risk management metric that estimates the maximum potential loss of a portfolio over a specific period, given a certain confidence level. It is used to assess the risk of extreme losses.

Value Stock: Value stocks are shares of companies that appear to be undervalued relative to their fundamentals, such as earnings, dividends, or sales. These stocks trade at a lower price than their intrinsic value, making them attractive to investors seeking to capitalize on potential price appreciation when the market recognizes the stock's true value.

Variance: Variance measures the dispersion of returns around the mean return, indicating the level of risk or uncertainty associated with an asset's price movements. It is the square of the standard deviation.

Vega: Vega measures the sensitivity of an option's price to changes in implied volatility. Higher vega implies greater sensitivity to volatility changes, which impacts the option's premium.

Vertical Credit Spread (Call / Put): A vertical credit spread involves selling an option and buying another option of the same type (call or put) with a different strike price but the same expiration date. It is used to generate income while limiting risk.

VIX: The VIX Index, also known as the "Volatility Index" or "Fear Gauge," measures the market's expectation of future volatility based on the prices of S&P 500 index options. A higher VIX indicates that traders expect significant price swings in the near future, often associated with increased uncertainty or fear in the market.

Volatility Skew: Volatility skew refers to the pattern observed in the implied volatilities of options across different strike prices. It reflects the market's perception of future volatility and risk, often indicating higher implied volatility for out-of-the-money options compared to at-the-money options. Volatility skew is commonly used to assess market sentiment and potential price movements.

Volatility Surface: The volatility surface is a three-dimensional plot that represents the implied volatilities of options across different strike prices and expiration dates. It provides a comprehensive view of market expectations for future volatility, allowing traders and analysts to assess how volatility varies with respect to moneyness and time to expiration.

W

Wheel Strategy: The wheel strategy involves selling cash-secured puts until assigned, then selling covered calls on the acquired stock. It is an income-generating strategy that cycles between selling puts and calls.

Z

Z-Score: A Z-score measures the number of standard deviations a data point is from the mean of a data set. It is used to assess the likelihood of a data point occurring within a normal distribution.

TABLE OF FIGURES

Figure 1 - Call Spread Payoff 16
Figure 2 - Put Spread Payoff 16
Figure 3 - Iron Condor Payoff 24
Figure 4 - Iron Butterfly Payoff 31
Figure 5 - Put Ratio Payoff 38
Figure 6 - Call Ratio Payoff... 38
Figure 7 - Short Strangle Payoff 44
Figure 8 - Short Straddle Payoff 52
Figure 9 - Collar Payoff 58
Figure 10 - Stock Repair Payoff 68
Figure 11 - Wheel Strategy Process 76
Figure 12 - Wheel Strategy Cash-Secured Put Payoff 77
Figure 13 - Wheel Strategy Covered Call Payoff 78
Figure 14 - Wheel Strategy With Put Credit Spread Payoff 102
Figure 15 - Wheel Strategy With Call Credit Spread Payoff............................. 102
Figure 16 - Wheel Strategy With Put Ratio Payoff 110
Figure 17 - Wheel Strategy With Call Ratio Payoff 111

TABLE OF TABLES

Table 1 - Cheat Sheet - Option Income Strategies 65
Table 2 - Wheel Strategies - Comparison 117

BIBLIOGRAPHY

Bittman, R. (1998). *Trading index options*. McGraw-Hill.

Black, F., & Scholes, M. (1973). *The Pricing of Options and Corporate Liabilities*. Journal of Political Economy, 81(3), 637-654.

Carmona, R. (2014). *Statistical Analysis of Financial Data in R*. Springer.

Chen, D. A., Sebastian, M. (2011). *The Option Trader's Hedge Fund: A Business Framework for Trading Equity and Index Options*. Wiley.

Cohen, G. (2005). *The Bible of Options Strategies: The Definitive Guide for Practical Trading Strategies*. FT Press.

Cottle, C. M. (2006). *Option Trading: The Hidden Reality*. RiskDoctor.

Fama, E. F., & French, K. R. (2004). *The Capital Asset Pricing Model: Theory and Evidence*. Journal of Economic Perspectives.

Gibbs, R. M. (2014). *Profiting from Weekly Options: How to Earn Consistent Income Trading Weekly Option Serials*. FT Press.

Hull, J. C. (2018). *Options, Futures, and Other Derivatives (10th ed.)*. Pearson.

Jabbour, G., Budwick, P. (2004). *The option trader handbook: Strategies and trade adjustments*. Wiley Trading.

Jensen, M. C. (1968). *The Performance of Mutual Funds in the Period 1945-1964*. Journal of Finance.

Johnston, S.A. (2003). *Trading Options to Win: Profitable Strategies and Tactics for Any Trader*. Wiley.

Kaufman, P. J. (2013). *Trading Systems and Methods (5th ed.)*. Wiley.

Kraft, B. (2009). *The smart investor's money machine: Methods and strategies to create regular income*. Wiley Trading.

Lowell, L. (2007). *Get Rich with Options: Four Winning Strategies Straight from the Exchange Floor*. Wiley.

McMillan, L. G. (2012). *Options as a Strategic Investment (5th ed.)*. Prentice Hall Press.

Nations, S. (2010). *The Complete Book of Option Spreads and Combinations: Strategies for Income Generation, Directional Moves, and Risk Reduction*. McGraw-Hill Education.

Passarelli, D. (2011), *The Market Taker's Edge*. McGrawHill

Reilly, F. K., & Brown, K. C. (2012). *Investment Analysis and Portfolio Management (10th ed.)*. South-Western College Pub.

Rhoads, R. (2008). *Option spread trading: A comprehensive guide to strategies and tactics*. Wiley Trading.

Saliba, A., J. (2009). *Option Spread Strategies: Trading Up, Down, and Sideways Markets*. Bloomberg Press.

Sebastian, M. (2021). *Trading Options for Edge: Profit from Options and Manage Risk like the Professionals*. McGraw-Hill Education.

Sharpe, W. F. (1964). *Capital Asset Prices: A Theory of Market Equilibrium under Conditions of Risk*. Journal of Finance.

Smith, C. D. (2008). *Option Strategies: Profit-Making Techniques for Stock, Stock Index, and Commodity Options*. Wiley.

Taleb, N. N. (2010). *The Black Swan: The Impact of the Highly Improbable (2nd ed.)*. Random House.

Wolff, J. (2013). *The Stock Option Income Generator: How to Make Steady Profits by Renting Your Stocks*. Wiley Trading.

Wolinsky, M. C. (2010). *Put Option Strategies for Smarter Trading: How to Protect and Build Capital in Turbulent Markets*. FT Press

Yates, L. (2003). *High Performance Options Trading: Option Volatility & Pricing Strategies*. Wiley.

Zerenner, E., Chupka, M. (2008). *Naked Puts: Power Strategies for Consistent Profits*. Marketplace Books.

Data Sources

Yahoo Finance: *https://finance.yahoo.com/*

Nasdaq: *https://www.nasdaq.com/*

www.ingramcontent.com/pod-product-compliance
Lightning Source LLC
Chambersburg PA
CBHW052301220526
45471CB00001B/442